KNOW YOUR FOE

In Search of an Enemy Within

Niyaz Harun Makhamalla

ISBN

Hardcase 979-8-89588-653-3
Paperback 979-8-89588-365-5

Contents

Contents

Acknowledgments

In writing "Know Your Foe - In Search of an Enemy Within," I am deeply grateful for the unwavering support and guidance of my family, who have played an instrumental role in my journey. To my parents, thank you for instilling in me the values of resilience, integrity, and perseverance. Your wisdom and encouragement have provided me with a solid foundation, allowing me to navigate life's challenges with confidence and clarity.

To my wife, your love and support have been my greatest strength. You inspire me daily with your kindness and understanding, and your belief in my vision has motivated me to pursue this project wholeheartedly. I am forever thankful for your companionship and the countless ways you uplift me.

My brother and sister-in-law, your insights and perspectives have been invaluable. You have always been there to offer guidance, share laughter, and remind me of the importance of family. The bond we share has enriched my life, and I cherish the moments we've spent together, celebrating both our successes and our struggles.

As a token of my love and appreciation, I dedicate this book to my daughter and niece. You are the future, and I hope that through this work, you find inspiration and strength in knowing your worth. May you always strive for self-awareness and authenticity, understanding that the greatest challenges often lie within. It is my wish that you embrace life with courage and curiosity, always seeking to know and conquer the foes that may arise.

This book is not only a reflection of my thoughts but also a tribute to my family's enduring love and guidance, which has shaped that I am today. Thank you all for being my anchors and my guiding stars.

Introduction

In life, there is perhaps no greater wisdom than truly understanding oneself and the world around us. One of the most significant facets of self-awareness is knowing your shortcomings—those areas where you might falter or be vulnerable. Equally important is recognizing the individuals, situations, or external forces that can cause harm, whether that harm comes in the form of mental, physical, financial, or moral damage. These two forms of awareness, self-knowledge and external vigilance, provide the foundation for personal growth, resilience, and the ability to navigate life's complexities.

The journey toward this understanding is not just an intellectual exercise but an ongoing process of introspection, experience, and vigilance. Many people live their lives without reflecting on their weaknesses, often to their detriment. Without knowing where our vulnerabilities lie, we expose ourselves to risks and dangers that could be mitigated with greater awareness. Moreover, the people and forces that can harm us are not always apparent. They may lurk in familiar faces or unexpected circumstances, and unless we are attuned to them, we remain susceptible to their influence.

The Importance of Self-Knowledge

The first step in this process is gaining a deep understanding of oneself. Self-knowledge involves identifying one's strengths, weaknesses, habits, and patterns of behaviour. It requires acknowledging uncomfortable truths, such as the traits that make us less effective or the tendencies that lead us to make poor decisions. This form of self-awareness is not just about listing out faults but involves an honest and critical reflection on how these shortcomings impact various aspects of life.

For instance, someone who is prone to procrastination might not only delay tasks but also face financial strain, career stagnation, or even relationship troubles. Recognizing this shortcoming is the first step in addressing it. The same goes for those who may have difficulty managing emotions. Without understanding how these traits affect one's mental state or decision-making, a person might struggle with interpersonal relationships or suffer from chronic stress and anxiety.

Self-awareness is also important in avoiding moral lapses. Each individual operates according to a personal ethical compass, but understanding where one might stray from that moral code is essential. For example, if someone knows they are susceptible to peer pressure or easily swayed by external influences, they can be more vigilant in situations where moral compromise is possible. This awareness prevents one from compromising values in exchange for short-term gain or social acceptance.

To develop self-knowledge, a person must engage in continuous self-reflection. This might involve regular introspection, journaling, or seeking feedback from trusted individuals. It also requires the willingness to accept criticism without defensiveness, which can be challenging but ultimately leads to growth. Moreover, mindfulness practices can help cultivate awareness of how one reacts to different stimuli, shedding light on unconscious behaviours or automatic responses that might contribute to poor decisions.

The Power of Knowing External Threats

While self-awareness is crucial, it is equally important to understand the external forces that can harm you. Life is filled with individuals and situations that can lead to harm, whether intentionally or unintentionally. Some of these threats are obvious, such as a dishonest business partner, an abusive relationship, or a hazardous work environment. However, many external threats are subtler and more insidious.

Mental harm can be inflicted by people who manipulate emotions, undermine confidence, or engage in gas lighting. Physical harm can come not only from direct violence but also from unhealthy lifestyle habits influenced by those around us. Financial harm can be inflicted through fraud, poor advice, or decisions driven by emotional impulses rather than rational thinking. Moral harm, while harder to quantify, is equally damaging. It can result from association with individuals who encourage unethical behaviour, erode moral judgment, or encourage compromising values for personal gain.

Recognizing these threats requires both intuition and knowledge. Intuition, or a gut feeling that something is amiss, often serves as an early warning system. However, relying solely on intuition without analysing the situation can lead to paranoia or false assumptions. Thus, it's essential to combine intuition with concrete knowledge and reasoning. Learning to read people and situations, understanding behavioural patterns, and researching the motivations of those around us can reveal potential harm that may not be immediately apparent.

For example, someone who always seems to take advantage of your generosity might be subtly draining your resources, both emotionally and financially, even though their actions might not appear malicious on the surface. Alternatively, a trusted colleague might have ulterior motives, quietly working to undermine your efforts in the workplace for their benefit. In either case, the threat is not immediately visible but becomes apparent over time through careful observation and reflection.

Additionally, understanding the broader environment—such as societal pressures, economic conditions, or political landscapes—helps in identifying external forces that may cause harm. Financial markets may be volatile, or political shifts might affect personal freedom or job security. By being aware of these larger external factors, one can make more informed decisions to safeguard against financial or social instability.

Mental and Emotional Resilience

Once you are aware of both your internal shortcomings and the external threats that may harm you, the next step is building mental and emotional resilience. Resilience is the ability to bounce back from setbacks, adapt to adversity, and continue moving forward despite challenges. It's not about avoiding harm entirely but rather about handling it effectively when it occurs.

Mental resilience comes from cultivating a mindset that embraces growth, self-improvement, and adaptability. This requires being open to change and accepting that failure and setbacks are part of the learning process. Resilient individuals do not allow failures to define them; instead, they use them as opportunities to learn and grow stronger.

Emotional resilience, on the other hand, involves developing the ability to regulate one's emotions, even in the face of stress, disappointment, or fear. Emotions can cloud judgment and lead to impulsive decisions, so being able to remain calm and clear-headed is crucial when dealing with external threats or addressing personal shortcomings.

In this regard, building a support network of trusted individuals is vital. Friends, family, mentors, and colleagues who understand your vulnerabilities can provide support, guidance, and feedback, helping you to navigate difficult situations and avoid potential harm. These relationships can also act as a buffer against emotional manipulation, providing a grounding force in situations where your emotions might otherwise get the best of you.

The Moral Dimension

Finally, understanding one's own shortcomings and external threats carries a moral dimension. Life is filled with ethical dilemmas, and knowing how to navigate them requires both self-awareness and an understanding of the moral implications of one's actions. For instance, failing to recognize how greed, envy, or pride might drive your decisions can lead to morally questionable actions. Likewise, associating with individuals who lack integrity can erode your ethical standards over time.

It's important to stay true to your moral compass even when faced with external pressures that tempt you to deviate. By identifying your moral vulnerabilities, you can fortify your ethical boundaries, making it more difficult for external forces to sway you from your principles. This not only protects your integrity but also ensures that you remain a force for good in the world, rather than someone who contributes to harm, whether intentionally or unintentionally.

Understanding your shortcomings and identifying those who can cause harm are vital skills for navigating life successfully. This knowledge allows you to protect yourself from mental, physical, financial, and moral harm while also fostering personal growth and resilience. The journey toward self-awareness and external vigilance is not an easy one, but it is essential for living a life that is not only fulfilling but also secure. By embracing this process, you create a foundation of strength and wisdom that enables you to face life's challenges with confidence and clarity.

The Dangers of Manipulation: Recognizing Hidden Agendas

In life, some individuals may seek to exploit others by sowing discord for their personal benefit, manipulating situations to create conflict. This form of manipulation is often subtle and insidious, but its effects can be deeply damaging, especially when the victim finds themselves embroiled in a conflict they never intended to engage in. Understanding how and why these manipulative tactics work—and knowing how to guard against them—is crucial for maintaining emotional and psychological well-being.

Manipulative individuals often thrive by creating confusion and playing on others' emotions. They may act as though they are concerned for your well-being, or they may cleverly present themselves as a trusted confidante. These people are experts at identifying emotional triggers and exploiting them. By presenting selective information, twisting facts, or even lying outright, they can subtly steer you into conflicts that serve their interests. For instance, they might frame a situation to make you believe someone has wronged you, when in reality; the entire narrative has been distorted. You, believing the information is true, may then act impulsively, confronting someone or starting a dispute.

By the time you realize that the conflict was based on false or exaggerated claims, it is often too late. The damage to relationships, trust, or reputations has already been done. In many cases, these manipulators sit back and watch the chaos unfold, benefitting from the division they have sown, while you are left wondering how you got involved in the conflict in the first place. This can leave you feeling disoriented and betrayed, both by the person you are now in conflict with and by the one who manipulated the situation.

There are several reasons why people engage in such behaviour. Sometimes, it's about power and control. By causing division and conflict, manipulators create a scenario where they can position themselves as indispensable or superior. They might offer to "mediate" the conflict they secretly initiated, gaining a position of influence in the process. In other cases, the motive might be jealousy or resentment. They may envy the harmony in your relationships or feel threatened by your success. Stirring up conflict can be their way of undermining your progress or isolating you from others.

Recognizing the signs of manipulation is the first step in protecting yourself. One common tactic is triangulation, where the manipulator pits two parties against each other without directly involving themselves. They may relay negative comments or half-truths, framing one person in a bad light to the other, all while maintaining their own appearance of neutrality or innocence. To guard against this, it's crucial to avoid reacting impulsively to second hand information. Instead, take time to verify the facts and consider the source. Ask yourself, "What does this person gain from telling me this?" or "Is there any evidence that supports their claims?"

Another red flag is when someone consistently stirs up drama or tension between others, yet never seems to be directly involved in the conflicts themselves. If someone always seems to be the messenger of bad news or negativity, this could be a sign that they are intentionally creating discord for their own benefit.

Conclusion

Being aware of manipulative individuals and their tactics can help you avoid unnecessary conflict and protect your mental and emotional well-being. By cultivating emotional intelligence, maintaining open and honest communication with others, and critically evaluating the motives behind someone's actions, you can shield yourself from being drawn into conflicts that serve someone else's agenda. The key is to stay vigilant and trust your instincts—when something doesn't feel right, it's often because it isn't.

The Power of Self-Integrity: Staying True to Your Principles

In life, we are often faced with decisions and situations where our principles are put to the test. Whether in personal relationships, at work, or in society, there will be times when the temptation to compromise your values or beliefs may arise. This could happen due to external pressures, lack of clarity, or the influence of people around you. However, as the saying goes, "Never compromise your own principles for something about which you don't have an idea." This statement reflects the importance of standing firm in your values, trusting your inner self, and having the courage to face challenges head-on without losing focus. Staying true to your principles is essential for personal growth, fulfilment, and long-term success.

The Importance of Principles

Principles are the core beliefs and values that guide your actions and decisions in life. They form the foundation of your character, providing you with a moral compass that helps you navigate the complexities of everyday life. Whether it's honesty, loyalty, respect, or kindness, these principles define who you are and what you stand for. When you hold fast to them, they give you direction, helping you make decisions that are consistent with your true self.

Compromising your principles can lead to inner conflict and regret. If you betray your own values for something you don't fully understand or believe in, it can leave you feeling lost, confused, or even ashamed.

On the other hand, standing by your principles, even when it's difficult or unpopular, leads to a sense of peace and self-respect. It empowers you to act with integrity and authenticity, which in turn builds trust and respect from others.

Stick to the Truth

The pursuit of truth is a cornerstone of integrity. In any situation, no matter how challenging, it's essential to remain truthful to yourself and others. The truth can sometimes be hard to face, but it is always the most solid ground to stand on. When you compromise on truth, you begin to drift away from your authentic self, which can lead to a life of confusion and instability.

Many times, people may pressure you to accept things that don't align with your beliefs or values, or they may ask you to take a stance on something about which you lack full knowledge or understanding. This is where the danger of compromising your principles comes in. In such situations, it's important to pause and reflect. If you don't fully understand something, there's no shame in admitting it. Instead of compromising, seek to learn more, ask questions, and investigate the truth before making a decision.

Truth serves as the bedrock for sound decisions and clear thinking. It helps you avoid being swayed by external forces or deceptive influences. In the long run, sticking to the truth enables you to build a life based on honesty and integrity, free from the complications of deceit or manipulation.

Trust Your Inner Self

One of the most powerful sources of guidance is your own inner self. Often referred to as intuition, your inner self is the voice of reason and wisdom that comes from within. It knows your deepest desires, your fears, and your values. When you are faced with difficult decisions or challenges, listening to your inner self can provide clarity and direction.

In a world filled with distractions, opinions, and external pressures, it's easy to lose sight of what truly matters to you. People may try to influence your decisions, but ultimately, no one knows you better than yourself. Trusting your inner self requires quiet reflection and self-awareness. It's about tuning out the noise of the world and listening to your own heart and mind.

However, trusting yourself does not mean ignoring the advice or perspectives of others. It means taking their input into account but making decisions that are aligned with your own principles and values. When you are true to yourself, you are better equipped to face challenges with confidence and resilience.

Have the Courage to Fight against the Odds

Life is full of challenges, obstacles, and adversities that test your resolve. At times, you may face situations where standing by your principles feels like an uphill battle. This is where courage comes into play. Courage is not the absence of fear, but the willingness to act despite it. It's the strength to uphold your values and beliefs, even when it's inconvenient, unpopular, or risky.

Having the courage to fight against the odds means being willing to stand alone if necessary. It means not compromising your integrity for the sake of convenience or acceptance. Courage allows you to confront challenges head-on, without wavering in your commitment to your values. Whether it's standing up for what is right in a difficult situation or resisting the pressure to conform, courage empowers you to stay focused on your goals and principles.

Beware of Those Who Distract You from Your Focus

In the pursuit of your goals and adherence to your principles, there will always be distractions. Some of these distractions may come in the form of people who intentionally or unintentionally steer you away from your focus. These individuals may not share your values or may have their own agenda that conflicts with yours.

It's essential to be mindful of who you allow into your inner circle. Surrounding yourself with people who support your growth, challenge you to stay true to your principles, and encourage your success is crucial. On the other hand, those who try to pull you away from your focus, either through negative influence or distraction, can derail your progress.

Stay vigilant and discerning when it comes to the people around you. Recognize when someone is leading you away from your goals or encouraging you to compromise on your principles. These distractions can come in many forms—temptations, toxic relationships, or even well-meaning advice that doesn't align with your values.

Conclusion

The journey of life is filled with challenges, temptations, and moments where your principles will be tested. However, staying true to your beliefs, seeking truth, and trusting your inner self can guide you through even the most difficult circumstances. Having the courage to face adversity and avoiding distractions from those who steer you away from your focus is essential for personal growth and fulfilment. Ultimately, no one knows you better than yourself, and when you remain steadfast in your values, you build a life rooted in integrity, purpose, and resilience.

III

The Importance of Ambition and the Danger of Negative Influences

Ambition is a driving force behind personal and professional success. It motivates us to achieve goals, strive for a better life, and improve ourselves in multiple ways—whether financially, physically, or socially. The statement warns against people who criticize those who seek to live a luxurious life, suggesting that such individuals may harbour their own insecurities or limiting beliefs. While it's true that money isn't everything, it undeniably plays an important role in achieving comfort, security, and freedom. Moreover, it argues that surrounding yourself with people who lack dreams and ambition can be detrimental to your own growth.

Money is Not Everything, but It's Something

It's often said that money can't buy happiness, but it's equally true that financial stability and success provide opportunities that make life easier and more enjoyable. Those who dismiss the pursuit of wealth or criticize others for living a comfortable or luxurious life are often speaking from a place of misunderstanding or judgment. While excessive materialism may indeed detract from more meaningful aspects of life, the responsible pursuit of financial success can enhance one's quality of life in numerous ways.

First and foremost, earning money through hard work brings a sense of accomplishment and independence. It allows individuals to make choices that align with their values and desires, whether that's travelling the world, investing in hobbies, supporting family or giving back to the community. A well-earned, comfortable life is not something to be ashamed of but rather a reflection of dedication, perseverance, and ambition.

Luxury, in this context, doesn't necessarily mean extravagant spending on unnecessary items. It can refer to having the freedom to pursue passions, live in a comfortable environment, and provide for loved ones. There's a distinction between wealth for wealth's sake and wealth as a tool to live a fulfilling life. It's important to recognize that financial success, when combined with other forms of well-being—such as health, relationships, and personal development—can create a balanced and meaningful life.

The Value of Ambition

Ambition is a powerful driver of success and progress. Without it, human potential remains untapped, and dreams remain unfulfilled. Ambition fuels the desire to improve, whether that's in career, personal life, health, or relationships. People with ambition not only strive to better themselves but also inspire those around them to do the same. They create momentum and are often the ones who bring about change, innovation, and growth in society.

Earning money is only one aspect of ambition. A truly successful person is also rich in health, meaningful relationships, and a strong social circle. The pursuit of wealth, therefore, should not come at the expense of these other important aspects of life. Health, both physical and mental, is essential for enjoying the fruits of one's labour. Likewise, friends and a good social circle provide support, joy, and perspective, making life richer in ways that money alone cannot.

A balanced life, therefore, includes ambition in all areas—earning money, maintaining health, building friendships, and nurturing a positive social environment. People who pursue growth in multiple areas are more likely to lead fulfilling, dynamic lives, and their success tends to radiate outward, positively affecting those around them.

Beware of the Dreamless

One of the key messages in the statement is to beware of people with no dreams or ambitions. These individuals can have a negative influence on your own mindset and goals. While it's natural to want to help or uplift others, consistently surrounding yourself with people who lack direction, motivation, or dreams can drain your energy and diminish your own ambitions. Their pessimism, lack of drive, or contentment with mediocrity can subtly influence your thoughts and actions, leading you to question your own goals or feel guilty about your successes.

People without dreams or ambitions may also discourage others from pursuing their own aspirations, either out of jealousy, fear, or a desire to justify their own inaction. They might make comments like, "Why work so hard when you could just take it easy?" or "Money doesn't buy happiness." While these statements might have some truth to them, they can also be used as excuses to avoid pushing boundaries, taking risks, or working towards something greater.

Moreover, people without ambitions can sometimes try to diminish the accomplishments of others in order to validate their own lack of progress. They may criticize those who strive for more, labelling them as greedy or materialistic. These judgments, however, are often a reflection of their own dissatisfaction with life. Instead of working on themselves or striving for improvement, they project their insecurities onto others who are trying to achieve success.

The Power of a Positive Circle

Just as people with no ambitions can bring you down, surrounding yourself with motivated, driven, and like-minded individuals can have the opposite effect. A good circle of friends and associates—one that shares your values, dreams, and ambitions—can provide invaluable support, encouragement, and inspiration. They challenge you to grow, celebrate your achievements, and push you to aim higher.

A positive social circle is one that recognizes the importance of ambition in all its forms—whether it's financial success, health goals, personal development, or fostering meaningful relationships. Such people understand that success is not one-dimensional, and they work to achieve balance in their own lives while encouraging you to do the same. Being part of a community of driven, successful people naturally elevates your own goals and ambitions, as you're constantly exposed to new ideas, opportunities, and perspectives.

Conclusion

In life, ambition is a vital ingredient for success, not just financially but in every aspect of well-being. While it's important to recognize that money isn't everything, it is certainly something—a means to a better, more fulfilling life. Ambition drives people to achieve their goals and live up to their potential, creating a life rich in health, friendships, and personal satisfaction.

It is equally important to be cautious of those who lack dreams and ambition. Such individuals can drain your energy and cause you to doubt your own aspirations. Instead, it's essential to surround yourself with like-minded, motivated people who encourage your growth and share your values. By maintaining ambition and cultivating a strong, positive social circle, you set yourself up for a balanced, successful, and fulfilling life.

IV

The Power of Independent Thinking: Navigating External Influences

In life, we often find ourselves surrounded by various opinions, beliefs, and advice from others. While some of these inputs may be well-intentioned, there are times when individuals or groups may try to influence us for their own benefit. This is why it is critical to develop and rely on your own independent thinking. The ability to form your own ideas, assess situations critically, and make decisions based on your values and judgment is one of the most powerful tools you can possess. The statement, "Never get influenced by others' thoughts. It may be they are trying to influence for their own benefit," highlights the importance of maintaining autonomy over your thought processes and resisting undue external pressure.

The Danger of External Influence

In today's fast-paced, hyper-connected world, external influence is everywhere. Social media, news outlets, advertising, and even the people closest to us can shape our perceptions and beliefs, sometimes without us realizing it. These influences can range from subtle suggestions to overt attempts to sway your thinking in a particular direction. While some influence can be positive—such as learning from mentors or considering different perspectives—others may be manipulative or self-serving.

People may attempt to influence you for various reasons. In personal relationships, someone might try to sway your opinions or decisions to meet their own emotional needs or desires. In professional settings, colleagues or superiors may try to influence your actions to gain a competitive advantage or further their own careers. On a societal level, marketers, politicians, and media outlets frequently use tactics to influence public opinion for financial gain or power.

The problem arises when you allow these influences to override your own independent thinking. You may find yourself making decisions or forming opinions based on what others want or expect from you, rather than what aligns with your own values, needs, and aspirations. Over time, this can lead to a loss of identity and personal direction, as you become more reactive to external inputs than proactive in shaping your own life.

The Importance of Critical Thinking

To avoid falling prey to external influence, it is crucial to develop and cultivate critical thinking skills. Critical thinking involves the ability to analyse information, question assumptions, and evaluate arguments or situations from multiple angles before reaching a conclusion. It empowers you to discern between right and wrong, and between ideas that serve your interests versus those that may serve someone else's.

In any situation where you feel you are being influenced by someone else's thoughts or ideas, it's important to pause and reflect. Ask yourself: "Is this person's opinion genuinely in my best interest? Are they trying to sway me for their own benefit? What do I really think about this situation, and how does it align with my values and goals?". By engaging in this type of reflective questioning, you create mental space to assess the situation more objectively and ensure that you are making choices that align with your authentic self.

Additionally, it's essential to gather information from multiple sources before forming an opinion. Relying on a single source of information or one person's perspective can limit your ability to see the full picture. When you actively seek diverse viewpoints, you enhance your capacity to think critically and make informed decisions. However, even as you gather different inputs, the ultimate decision should always be yours—one based on thoughtful reflection and an understanding of your core values.

The Role of Self-Confidence in Independent Thinking

One of the main reasons people are susceptible to external influence is a lack of self-confidence. When you doubt your own ideas or judgment, it becomes easy to defer to others who appear more confident or authoritative. However, building confidence in your own thought process is key to resisting undue influence.

Self-confidence comes from trusting your ability to think, analyse, and make decisions. This doesn't mean you will always be right—mistakes are a natural part of learning and growth—but it means having faith in your own capacity to learn from experiences and adjust your thinking accordingly. When you develop self-confidence, you are less likely to feel pressured to conform to others' expectations or ideas. Instead, you stand firm in your beliefs and are open to adapting them when necessary, based on your own insights, not external pressure.

Building self-confidence also requires self-awareness. When you have a strong understanding of your own values, goals, and motivations, you are better equipped to make decisions that are authentic to you. This self-awareness acts as a compass, guiding you through situations where external influences might try to pull you in different directions. It allows you to remain grounded, even in the face of conflicting opinions or pressures.

The Power of Original Ideas

Independent thinking is not just about resisting external influence; it's also about cultivating original ideas and innovative solutions. When you rely solely on others' thoughts, you limit your creativity and potential for innovation. The most successful and fulfilled individuals are often those who think outside the box, who aren't afraid to challenge the status quo, and who come up with novel ideas that reflect their unique perspective on the world.

By fostering your own thought process, you create room for originality. You become a creator of ideas rather than a passive consumer of others' beliefs. Whether it's in your personal life, your career, or your creative pursuits, the ability to generate and act on your own ideas is a powerful form of self-expression and empowerment. It not only sets you apart from the crowd but also leads to personal fulfilment, as you pursue paths that resonate with your true self rather than following a script written by others.

Avoiding the Influence of Those with Hidden Agendas

Lastly, the statement cautions against people who might influence you for their own benefit. These individuals often have hidden agendas and may use manipulation or persuasion to serve their own interests at your expense. It is important to remain vigilant in these situations, always questioning the motivations behind someone else's advice or opinions.

Surround yourself with people who respect your independence of thought and encourage you to develop your own ideas. Seek out mentors and peers who offer guidance without imposing their views on you, and who help you think critically rather than simply telling you what to do.

Conclusion

In a world full of external influences, staying true to your own thought process and ideas is essential for personal growth, integrity, and success. While it's natural to seek advice or input from others, it's important to filter these through the lens of your own judgment and values. Critical thinking, self-awareness, and self-confidence are key components of independent thinking, empowering you to make decisions that align with your authentic self. By cultivating these skills and resisting undue external influence, you can lead a life that is guided by your own principles and ambitions, rather than the expectations or agendas of others.

V

The Importance of Recognizing and Guarding Your Weaknesses

Self-awareness is a cornerstone of personal growth and success. One of the most crucial aspects of self-awareness is recognizing your own weaknesses. The statement emphasizes not only the need to identify and work on personal weaknesses but also to keep them private, as exposing them can make you vulnerable to manipulation or harm. In a world where people may take advantage of others for personal gain, guarding your weaknesses is a strategy for self-preservation and empowerment.

The Power of Self-Awareness

Self-awareness is the ability to understand your own thoughts, emotions, strengths, and weaknesses. It allows you to critically assess your behavior and make adjustments where necessary. The first step to improving any weakness is acknowledging that it exists. Many people tend to shy away from recognizing their flaws because it can be uncomfortable or humbling. However, ignoring your weaknesses doesn't make them disappear—it simply leaves you unprepared to address them when they arise.

By understanding your weaknesses, you take control of them rather than allowing them to control you. Self-awareness grants you the power to turn weaknesses into strengths by actively working to improve them. For example, if you recognize that you struggle with time management, you can take deliberate steps to improve this skill—such as using tools like planners, setting reminders, or delegating tasks. Without this recognition, you would continue to be inefficient and stressed, without realizing the root cause of your problem.

Working on Your Weaknesses

Identifying your weaknesses is only the first step. The real work begins when you commit to improving them. No one is without flaws, but the difference between those who succeed and those who don't often lies in the willingness to confront and work on these areas. Strengthening your weak points can lead to greater overall competence and confidence.

This process requires discipline, patience, and a willingness to make changes. You might need to seek external help—such as coaching, training, or mentorship—to effectively address certain weaknesses. For instance, if public speaking is a weakness, joining a speaking club or taking a course can help build confidence and skill in this area. By consistently working on your weaknesses, you gradually diminish their power over your life and career.

In the professional world, recognizing and improving weaknesses can make you more competitive. Many successful leaders acknowledge that their ability to continually self-reflect and improve is what sets them apart. They don't shy away from challenges but actively seek to overcome their limitations. This growth mindset allows them to turn potential weaknesses into strengths over time.

Keeping Your Weaknesses Private

While it's important to work on your weaknesses, it's equally critical to keep them private. Revealing your weaknesses to others can leave you vulnerable to exploitation. In competitive environments—whether in business, politics, or even social relationships—there will always be individuals who might use your vulnerabilities to their advantage. This could manifest as manipulation, sabotage, or even bullying.

For example, in a workplace setting, if a colleague knows you have trouble managing stress, they might try to overwhelm you with tasks or responsibilities, hoping you will falter. In a negotiation, if your counterpart knows that you struggle with assertiveness, they may push harder to get the upper hand, knowing you're less likely to stand firm on your demands. By keeping your weaknesses private, you maintain a level of control over how others perceive and interact with you.

Emotional Intelligence and Managing Perceptions

Emotional intelligence plays a crucial role in how you manage and conceal your weaknesses. People with high emotional intelligence are adept at understanding not only their own emotions but also the emotions of others. They can regulate their responses to stressful situations, making it harder for others to exploit their vulnerabilities.

One aspect of emotional intelligence is the ability to project confidence, even when you are uncertain or insecure about something. This doesn't mean pretending to be invincible, but rather controlling the narrative about you. If you know that a particular area is a weakness, such as handling criticism or managing pressure, you can develop strategies to mask this vulnerability. For example, you might practice deflecting criticism with humor or calming yourself during high-pressure situations through mindfulness techniques.

Additionally, managing how others perceive you can help protect your weaknesses. In professional and social environments, people often make judgments based on behavior and communication. If you are aware of a weakness, you can consciously work to present yourself in ways that minimize its impact. For example, if you know that you struggle with indecision, you might train yourself to appear more decisive in meetings by preparing thoroughly in advance and speaking with confidence, even if you are unsure. This gives the impression of control and competence, preventing others from detecting your internal doubts.

Guarding Against Manipulation

People who are aware of your weaknesses may use them against you for their own benefit. This can happen subtly, through manipulation, or more overtly, through power plays or confrontation. When someone knows your vulnerabilities, they have a psychological advantage, as they can push your emotional buttons, create stress, or put you in situations where you are more likely to make mistakes.

To prevent this, it's essential to build defenses around your weaknesses by maintaining boundaries and not giving away too much information about yourself. In professional settings, be cautious about revealing personal details or admitting to struggles unless you're in a trusted, safe environment. Even in personal relationships, it's important to consider whether someone has your best interests at heart before exposing your vulnerabilities.

Furthermore, strengthening your emotional resilience can help protect you from those who might attempt to exploit your weaknesses. By developing coping strategies and building your self-esteem, you make it harder for others to manipulate or undermine you.

Conclusion: Mastery of Self and Protection from Exploitation

Recognizing and working on your weaknesses is a powerful form of self-mastery. It allows you to become stronger, more capable, and less susceptible to being thrown off course by challenges. However, it's equally important to guard those weaknesses from public view, as exposing them can make you vulnerable to manipulation or harm.

By cultivating self-awareness, emotional intelligence, and a strategic approach to personal growth, you can protect yourself from external threats while improving your overall effectiveness. The balance lies in being honest with yourself about where you need improvement, working diligently to address those areas, and ensuring that others cannot use them to their advantage. This thoughtful and balanced approach to managing weaknesses not only strengthens your character but also shields you from the risks that come from revealing too much.

VI

Letting Go of the Past: Embracing the Present for Growth and Progress

The past holds a significant place in our lives, filled with experiences—both good and bad—that shape who we are. However, there comes a point when focusing too much on the past can hinder personal growth and progress. The statement encourages us to acknowledge our past, learn from it, but not let it dictate our present. Dwelling on the past can be one of the greatest barriers to success and self-fulfillment, while focusing on the present allows us to grow, move forward, and become the best versions of ourselves.

To begin, it's important to recognize that the past is unchangeable. The moments, decisions, and events that have already transpired are set in stone. No amount of reflection or regret can alter what has occurred. This is why clinging to the past, especially the negative experiences, can be emotionally draining and counterproductive. If we constantly ruminate over mistakes or missed opportunities, we are essentially living in a time that no longer exists. This prevents us from fully engaging with the present moment, where real change and growth happen.

The statement wisely advises us to focus on the present, emphasizing that it is the key to progress. The present is where you have the power to act, make decisions, and shape your future. Unlike the past, the present offers opportunities for growth, learning, and improvement. Every moment provides a fresh slate, where you can take steps toward your goals and create the life you want to live. By grounding yourself in the present, you harness your potential and make progress, regardless of past failures or setbacks.

However, this doesn't mean that the past should be completely forgotten. The past, after all, offers valuable lessons. Each mistake, triumph, and experience serves as a teacher, guiding us in how to navigate the present and future. Reflecting on your past can help you recognize patterns, understand what worked and what didn't, and develop strategies to avoid repeating the same mistakes. For instance, a failed relationship might teach you important lessons about communication or boundaries, while a missed career opportunity could sharpen your focus and determination moving forward.

The key, though, is not to let these lessons weigh you down. Learning from the past doesn't mean becoming stuck in it. You must extract the wisdom from your experiences without letting them define you or limit your present actions. It's about finding the balance between reflection and release. Those who fixate on past failures often end up paralyzed by fear or regret, unable to take risks or pursue new opportunities because they are haunted by what went wrong before. This mindset can sabotage growth and stifle progress.

Similarly, people who are overly attached to their past successes may also find themselves stuck. They might resist change, clinging to outdated methods or ideas because they worked before, even though the world around them is evolving. This can lead to stagnation, as they fail to adapt to new circumstances or embrace innovation. Whether your past is filled with failures or triumphs, the most important thing is to acknowledge that it is behind you and that the present is where your true power lies.

Sticking to the past, especially its negative aspects can be particularly harmful because it creates a mental loop that fosters self-doubt, guilt, and frustration. When you allow your mind to dwell on what could have been or what went wrong, you're essentially giving your energy to something that no longer exists. This is why the statement identifies your biggest enemy as your own fixation on the past. This self-imposed barrier keeps you from seeing new possibilities or appreciating the opportunities right in front of you.

To break free from this mental trap, it's crucial to develop mindfulness and emotional intelligence. Mindfulness, which involves being fully present in the moment, helps you shift your focus away from the past and center it on what's happening now. Practicing mindfulness can enhance your ability to appreciate the present and recognize that each day is a new opportunity to grow. By learning to stay present, you gradually let go of the past's hold on you, freeing up your mental and emotional energy for current challenges and opportunities.

Emotional intelligence, on the other hand, involves understanding and managing your emotions, especially those tied to past experiences. It allows you to acknowledge your feelings about the past without being controlled by them. For example, it's natural to feel regret or disappointment over past failures, but emotional intelligence helps you process those emotions constructively rather than letting them dominate your thinking. Through emotional intelligence, you can transform past pain into motivation for improvement, using the lessons learned as tools for growth.

Another important aspect of focusing on the present is setting goals and taking actionable steps toward them. When you are fully immersed in your present goals, there's less room to dwell on the past. Setting clear, achievable goals helps direct your energy and attention toward creating a better future. This forward-thinking approach encourages personal development, making it easier to let go of the past and embrace what's happening now.

In addition, surrounding yourself with positive influences and maintaining a support system can reinforce your ability to stay present. Friends, family, or mentors who encourage growth and progress can help keep you grounded in the present and focused on the future. They can also offer perspective when you find yourself slipping back into negative thinking about the past. A strong support system serves as a reminder that your life is constantly evolving, and that the best is yet to come as long as you remain focused on the present.

In conclusion, while the past may hold valuable lessons, it is the present that offers the real opportunity for growth and progress. Dwelling on past mistakes or successes can be one of the greatest barriers to personal fulfillment, as it limits your ability to engage with the present moment where change is possible. By learning from the past without letting it control you, practicing mindfulness, and focusing on actionable goals, you can free yourself from the weight of the past and move forward with confidence and purpose. The present is the only time where you have the power to act, and by embracing it, you allow yourself to grow, improve, and progress toward the future you desire.

VII

The Hidden Enemy of Emotional Capitalization: How Seeking Sympathy Weakens Confidence

Emotions are a natural part of being human. We all experience highs and lows, moments of joy and sorrow, excitement and frustration. However, the way we manage and express these emotions, especially in public or social settings, has a significant impact on how we are perceived by others and how we perceive ourselves. The statement "Never capitalize your emotions in front of everyone to gain sympathy from others" serves as a reminder of the risks associated with publicly displaying emotional vulnerability for the sake of eliciting sympathy. While expressing emotions is healthy, capitalizing on them for attention can, in the long run, erode your confidence and create a hidden enemy within.

Emotional Capitalization: A Dangerous Trap

Emotional capitalization refers to the act of deliberately displaying your emotions, particularly negative ones, to gain sympathy, attention, or validation from others. It can manifest in various forms, such as constantly talking about personal hardships, exaggerating challenges, or frequently seeking reassurance. While it may initially seem like a way to build connections or receive support, emotional capitalization often backfires.

One of the dangers of this behavior is that it fosters dependency on external validation. When you rely on others' sympathy to feel valued or understood, you give away your emotional power. Your sense of self-worth becomes tied to how others respond to your emotional expressions. Over time, this can make you emotionally dependent on others, weakening your ability to handle challenges on your own and diminishing your self-confidence. You begin to question your strength, wondering whether you are truly capable of overcoming obstacles without external support.

In addition to weakening your self-confidence, emotional capitalization can lead to a distorted self-perception. By constantly sharing your struggles with others, you reinforce a narrative of helplessness or victimhood. This narrative becomes internalized, causing you to view yourself as someone who is always in need of help, rather than someone capable of overcoming difficulties. As a result, you may start to believe that you are weaker than you actually are which further diminishes your confidence and self-esteem.

The Social Cost of Emotional Capitalization

Apart from the internal damage emotional capitalization causes, it also has social consequences. Initially, people may respond to your emotional displays with compassion and sympathy. However, over time, constant expressions of vulnerability can lead to sympathy fatigue. People may begin to see you as someone who is emotionally needy or dependent, and this can strain relationships. Instead of being viewed as strong and resilient, you may be seen as someone who lacks emotional stability and the ability to manage life's challenges independently.

Moreover, relying on sympathy can create an unbalanced dynamic in your relationships. When you consistently seek sympathy, you place others in the role of emotional caretaker. While occasional emotional support is normal and healthy in close relationships, constantly relying on others to validate your feelings can create a burden for them. They may start to feel obligated to provide reassurance and support, even when they are emotionally drained themselves. This dynamic can lead to resentment and distance in relationships, as others may pull away to protect their emotional well-being.

In professional settings, emotional capitalization can be particularly detrimental. In the workplace, where competence, reliability, and resilience are valued, displaying vulnerability to gain sympathy can harm your reputation. Colleagues or supervisors may perceive you as someone who is not capable of handling stress or difficult situations. This perception can hinder your career progression, as you may not be considered for leadership roles or challenging projects. While emotional intelligence and vulnerability have their place in the workplace, constantly seeking sympathy can signal emotional instability, which can undermine your professional credibility.

The Hidden Enemy: Eroding Confidence

Perhaps the most insidious effect of emotional capitalization is how it erodes your internal confidence. When you seek sympathy from others, you subtly reinforce the idea that you are not strong enough to handle challenges on your own. Over time, this mindset becomes a self-fulfilling prophecy. You start to doubt your ability to navigate difficult situations independently, and as a result, your confidence weakens.

Confidence comes from a sense of self-reliance and trust in your abilities. When you consistently look to others for validation, you lose the opportunity to build that trust in yourself. Instead of confronting challenges and developing resilience, you rely on external emotional support, which prevents you from growing stronger. This reliance on sympathy can become a hidden enemy because it undermines your belief in your own strength. You may not even realize how much your confidence is being chipped away until you find yourself struggling to cope without external reassurance.

Embracing Emotional Strength: The Alternative to Sympathy-Seeking

The alternative to emotional capitalization is cultivating emotional strength. This doesn't mean suppressing your emotions or pretending to be unaffected by difficulties. Instead, it means learning how to process and manage your emotions in a way that strengthens your resilience and builds your confidence.

1. **Self-Awareness:** Developing self-awareness is the first step toward emotional strength. Recognize when you are seeking sympathy and ask yourself why. Are you feeling insecure or overwhelmed? Are you looking for validation because you don't believe you can handle the situation on your own? By becoming aware of these patterns, you can begin to break free from the cycle of sympathy-seeking.

2. **Internal Validation:** Instead of relying on others for validation, practice validating your own emotions. Acknowledge your feelings without judgment, and remind yourself that it's okay to feel upset or vulnerable. The key is to recognize that you have the strength to cope with these emotions without needing external reassurance. Over time, this practice will help you build internal confidence and emotional resilience.

3. **Developing Emotional Coping Skills:** Learn healthy ways to cope with difficult emotions, such as stress, sadness, or frustration. Techniques like mindfulness, journaling, or talking to a trusted friend (without seeking sympathy) can help you process your emotions constructively. By developing your

emotional coping skills, you'll become more self-reliant and less dependent on others for emotional support.

4. **Strengthening Resilience:** Resilience comes from confronting challenges head-on and learning how to navigate them independently. Instead of focusing on your emotional struggles, focus on finding solutions to the problems at hand. By shifting your mindset from victimhood to empowerment, you build the resilience needed to handle future challenges with confidence.

Conclusion: Protecting Your Confidence

While emotions are a natural and important part of life, capitalizing on them for sympathy is a hidden enemy that can weaken your confidence and damage your relationships. The key to emotional strength is finding a balance between expressing your emotions and maintaining your independence. By cultivating self-awareness, internal validation, and resilience, you can build a stronger, more confident version of yourself. In doing so, you protect your confidence from being eroded by the need for external validation, and you become better equipped to face life's challenges with courage and strength.

VIII

The Power of Protecting Your Mind: Escaping Toxic Environments and Embracing Solitude

Surrounding yourself with the right people is one of the most crucial decisions you can make in life. The people you spend time with have a significant influence on your thoughts, emotions, and overall well-being. If those around you harbor dark, negative thoughts or ideas, they can easily drag you into their toxic mindset, distorting your perspective on life. The advice to distance yourself from such environments and embrace solitude—or seek healthier surroundings—is not only practical but essential for personal growth and mental health. At the end of the day, you must recognize that, in many ways, you are on your own in this journey, responsible for protecting your mind and well-being.

The Influence of Negative Surroundings

Humans are inherently social creatures and the people around us—whether friends, family, or colleagues—play a pivotal role in shaping our worldview. This phenomenon is often referred to as social influence, where the behaviors, attitudes, and thoughts of those around us subtly (or sometimes overtly) shape our own. While social influence can be positive when you are surrounded by optimistic, supportive, and driven people, it can quickly become harmful when those people harbor negativity, bitterness, or destructive ideas.

Negative environments can manifest in various ways. Sometimes, they involve individuals who are perpetually cynical, pessimistic, or consumed by dark thoughts. They may constantly talk about what's wrong in the world, focus on limitations rather than possibilities, or engage in destructive behaviors like gossip, jealousy, or even illegal activities. In other cases, the toxicity may be less overt, manifesting as subtle manipulations, discouragement, or emotional drain. Over time, exposure to these dark energies can erode your mental health, drain your motivation, and cloud your vision for the future. Worse still, the longer you remain in such surroundings, the more likely you are to adopt these negative thought patterns yourself, often without realizing it.

This is why it's essential to be mindful of the company you keep. If you find that those around you often speak of hopelessness, engage in self-sabotaging behaviors, or encourage negative thinking, it's a sign that their influence could be damaging your well-being. The longer you stay in such an environment, the harder it becomes to maintain a positive mindset and make progress in life. It's like being in a boat surrounded by people drilling holes in the floor; eventually, you all sink. To protect yourself from this downward spiral, it's vital to distance yourself from such environments.

The Strength in Solitude

When faced with negative surroundings, one of the most powerful steps you can take is to embrace solitude. While society often portrays being alone as something to be avoided—equating it with loneliness— solitude, when used constructively, can be a source of incredible strength. Time spent alone allows you to disconnect from external influences and reconnect with yourself, your values, and your goals. It gives you the space to think clearly, reflect on your life, and make decisions without the noise and distractions of others' opinions.

Solitude also provides an opportunity for introspection and self-discovery. In the stillness, you can examine your thoughts, confront your fears, and gain a deeper understanding of what truly matters to you. This process of self-reflection is vital for personal growth, as it allows you to identify areas of improvement, set meaningful goals, and develop a stronger sense of self. When you're constantly surrounded by other people, it can be difficult to hear your inner voice—solitude gives you the silence needed to listen.

Moreover, learning to be comfortable in your own company fosters independence and resilience. When you no longer rely on others for validation or guidance, you become more self-sufficient, capable of navigating life's challenges with confidence. This self-reliance is crucial, especially when the people around you are not supportive or share dark thoughts. It empowers you to trust your judgment, make decisions that are in your best interest, and avoid being swayed by the negativity of others.

Seeking Positive Surroundings

While solitude is a powerful tool for self-preservation and growth, it's also important to recognize that humans need connection and companionship. However, the key is to seek out relationships and environments that are uplifting, encouraging, and aligned with your values. Surrounding yourself with people who share your aspirations, who challenge you to be better, and who maintain a positive outlook on life can profoundly impact your personal development.

Positive environments fuel growth by encouraging a mindset of possibility and abundance. When you are around people who believe in themselves and in you, who celebrate your successes and support your journey, you are more likely to stay motivated and focused on your goals. These individuals provide constructive feedback, push you out of your comfort zone, and serve as examples of what's possible when you maintain a healthy, optimistic perspective. In such environments, you are not only supported in your growth but are also held accountable for staying true to your values and ambitions.

Finding such positive surroundings may require effort and discernment. It could mean seeking new friendships, joining groups or communities that align with your interests, or distancing yourself from long-standing relationships that have become toxic. It may feel difficult at first, especially if you've been part of a negative environment for a long time, but the benefits of surrounding yourself with positive influences far outweigh the discomfort of making these changes.

You Are On Your Own: The Reality of Personal Responsibility

The statement, "you are on your own," carries a bittersweet truth: while you may have friends, family, or colleagues, at the end of the day, you are the one responsible for your own life. No one else can make decisions for you, and no one else will bear the consequences of your choices as deeply as you will. Recognizing this reality is empowering because it places control in your hands. You have the power to choose who you surround yourself with, how you spend your time, and what kind of energy you allow into your life.

While the journey of self-discovery and self-improvement can sometimes feel isolating, especially when distancing yourself from toxic environments, it's also an opportunity to cultivate resilience and inner strength. The realization that you are on your own teaches you that you are enough, that you are capable of standing strong even in solitude, and that you have the power to create a better life for yourself by making conscious decisions about your environment.

Conclusion

In summary, the importance of protecting your mind from negative environments cannot be overstated. Surrounding yourself with people who harbor dark thoughts or ideas can erode your confidence and prevent you from living your best life. While solitude may seem daunting, it offers a valuable opportunity for reflection, growth, and self-reliance. Ultimately, embracing this solitude, or seeking healthier, more positive surroundings, will enable you to thrive. And though the journey is yours alone, it is one that can lead to greater strength, clarity, and success.

IX

Creating a Cheerful Home: A Sanctuary for Mental Well-Being

A home is more than just a physical space; it's an emotional and mental sanctuary that profoundly impacts the well-being of its inhabitants. The environment within a home should be cheerful, fostering positivity and mental health for everyone who lives there. As the statement suggests, when life's basic needs—food, shelter, clothing, and health—is provided, there's no reason why a home shouldn't also be a place of happiness, comfort, and peace. A cheerful home can be the foundation for emotional stability, personal growth, and a sense of belonging, enhancing the lives of all who dwell within it.

The Importance of a Cheerful Environment

The atmosphere in your personal space or home has a direct influence on your mental and emotional state. A home that radiates warmth, positivity, and cheerfulness helps reduce stress, anxiety, and tension. It serves as a refuge from the outside world, where challenges and hardships may constantly arise. Within a cheerful home, individuals can recharge, heal, and build the resilience necessary to face life's difficulties. On the other hand, a home filled with negativity, conflict, or gloom can do the opposite—exacerbating mental strain, leading to burnout, and negatively affecting relationships.

When God has provided you with the essentials—two meals a day, a roof over your head, clothing, and good health—it becomes your responsibility to cultivate an environment that reflects gratitude for these blessings. Often, people focus solely on material wealth or external success as measures of a happy life. While financial security is important, the true essence of happiness begins at home. When your home is filled with peace and cheer, the material and physical blessings you have are enjoyed to their fullest.

Cultivating a Cheerful Atmosphere

So, what does it take to create a cheerful and happy home environment? The first step is fostering positive relationships within the household. The people you share your space with play a crucial role in shaping the emotional climate of your home. Encouraging open communication, mutual respect, and understanding helps create an atmosphere where everyone feels valued and heard. When conflicts arise, as they naturally do, resolving them with patience and kindness ensures that negativity doesn't fester and grow into something more damaging. By prioritizing harmony and empathy, you can maintain a positive and supportive household.

In addition to healthy relationships, the physical aspects of the home also play a role in creating a cheerful environment. A well-maintained, clean, and organized space can significantly enhance the mood and mental state of the people living there. The arrangement of furniture, colors on the walls, and the overall decor of the home can affect how cheerful it feels. Bright colors, natural light, and fresh air all contribute to a lively and uplifting environment. Plants, artwork, and personal touches that reflect the personalities of the residents can also create a more inviting and warm space. When you take care of your living environment, it reflects your inner state and promotes mental well-being.

Another important element of a cheerful home is the presence of shared activities and moments of joy. Whether it's sharing a meal together, engaging in family traditions, or simply spending quality time with one another, these moments create bonds and memories that bring happiness into the household. Celebrating small victories, showing gratitude, and practicing kindness toward each other can also foster a cheerful atmosphere. When everyone in the household actively contributes to creating positivity, the home becomes a place of joy and comfort for all.

Gratitude and Contentment

Central to the idea of a cheerful home is the practice of gratitude. When you recognize the blessings in your life—whether it's having enough food to eat, a roof over your head or the good health to enjoy life— this perspective naturally fosters a sense of contentment. Gratitude helps shift the focus from what you don't have to what you do have, which can significantly improve your overall happiness. When you acknowledge and appreciate these basic blessings, it becomes easier to create an environment that reflects that joy.

A home rooted in gratitude will always be a place of positivity, regardless of external circumstances. Life will always bring challenges, but when your home is built on a foundation of thankfulness, it becomes a source of strength. Gratitude helps you maintain a cheerful outlook, even during difficult times. It encourages a mindset that sees the glass as half full, and this positivity spreads to everyone in the household.

Protecting the Home from Negativity

While it's important to cultivate a cheerful environment, it's equally essential to protect that environment from negativity. Negative influences, whether they come from outside the home or within, can quickly erode the peace and happiness you've worked to create. One common source of negativity is stress—whether from work, financial pressures, or personal challenges. It's important to manage stress effectively and prevent it from spilling into the home environment.

Setting boundaries between work and personal life, practicing relaxation techniques, and encouraging open conversations about stress can help keep negativity at bay.

In addition, it's important to be mindful of the media and entertainment consumed within the home. While it's easy to overlook, constant exposure to negative news, violent entertainment, or toxic social media can have a subtle but significant impact on the mood of the household. Balancing these with positive, uplifting content can help maintain the cheerful atmosphere you're aiming for.

A Home for Mental and Emotional Well-being

At its core, a cheerful home is one that promotes mental and emotional well-being. It's a space where individuals feel safe, supported, and understood. It's where personal growth happens, where family bonds are strengthened, and where challenges are faced with optimism and resilience. When the home is cheerful, it serves as a foundation for success in other areas of life. It becomes easier to pursue goals, overcome obstacles, and maintain a positive outlook on life.

In conclusion, a cheerful home is not only a blessing but also a choice. While external circumstances may fluctuate, the atmosphere within your home is something you can control. By fostering positive relationships, maintaining a well-kept space, practicing gratitude, and protecting your home from negativity, you can create a sanctuary that nurtures the mental and emotional well-being of everyone who lives there. When God has provided you with the essentials of life, it's your responsibility to make your home a place of happiness and cheer—a place where everyone can thrive.

X

The Hidden Enemy Within: Understanding and Managing Unnecessary Anger

Anger is a powerful emotion that, when left unchecked, can become a hidden enemy within ourselves. While it is a natural human response to certain situations, unnecessary anger can lead to both emotional and physical damage. It can affect our relationships, hinder our personal growth, and even lead to serious health issues. Furthermore, in a world where interpersonal dynamics are complex, our anger can be exploited by others, leading to further complications in our lives. Understanding the nature of anger and learning to manage it is crucial for maintaining our mental and emotional well-being.

Anger often arises as a reaction to perceived injustices or frustrations. When we feel threatened, wronged, or disrespected, our immediate response may be to lash out or express our anger. While some anger can be justified—acting as a catalyst for change or a signal that something is wrong—much of the anger we experience is unnecessary. It is often rooted in misunderstandings, miscommunication, or unrealistic expectations. This unnecessary anger can manifest in various ways, from mild irritation to explosive rage, and can have detrimental effects on our mental health.

One of the most significant emotional damages caused by unnecessary anger is the strain it puts on our relationships. When we allow anger to control our responses, we risk alienating the people around us. Friends, family members, and colleagues may feel uncomfortable or threatened by our outbursts, leading to tension and conflict. Over time, this can erode trust and intimacy in our relationships, leaving us isolated and unsupported. The people we care about may distance themselves to protect their own emotional well-being, leaving us in a cycle of loneliness and frustration.

In addition to the emotional toll, unnecessary anger can lead to physical damage as well. Chronic anger is linked to a range of health issues, including high blood pressure, cardiovascular disease, and weakened immune function. The body's stress response is activated during anger, releasing hormones like adrenaline and cortical. While this response can be useful in short bursts, prolonged exposure to these hormones can have harmful effects on our physical health. Furthermore, individuals who struggle with anger may be more prone to engage in unhealthy coping mechanisms, such as substance abuse, overeating, or other destructive behaviors, further exacerbating the damage to their health.

Moreover, our anger can be used as weapon by others. People who recognize that we have a tendency to become angry may deliberately provoke us to gain control in a situation or manipulate our reactions. This is particularly common in competitive environments, whether in personal relationships or the workplace. By exploiting our anger, others can shift the focus away from their own shortcomings or wrongdoings, placing us in a position where we are defending ourselves instead of addressing the real issues at hand. In this way, unnecessary anger can become a double-edged sword, harming us while simultaneously providing others with leverage over us.

To combat unnecessary anger, it is essential to develop self-awareness and emotional intelligence. Recognizing the triggers that lead to our anger is the first step in managing it effectively. By understanding what situations, people, or experiences provoke our anger, we can work to address these issues more constructively. This might involve taking a step back to assess the situation, seeking clarification through communication, or developing strategies to cope with frustration in healthier ways.

Practicing mindfulness can also be a powerful tool in managing anger. Mindfulness involves staying present in the moment and observing our thoughts and feelings without judgment. By developing a mindfulness practice, we can create a space between the stimulus that triggers our anger and our response to it. This allows us to respond more thoughtfully and deliberately rather than reacting impulsively. Techniques such as deep breathing, meditation, or journaling can help cultivate mindfulness and promote emotional regulation.

In addition, learning to communicate effectively can help reduce unnecessary anger in our interactions. Often, our anger stems from misunderstandings or miscommunications. By honing our communication skills, we can express our feelings more clearly and assertively, minimizing the likelihood of conflict. Using "I" statements, for example, allows us to articulate our feelings without placing blame on others, reducing defensiveness and promoting healthier discussions.

Setting boundaries is also crucial in managing anger. It is essential to identify the situations or relationships that provoke our anger and establish clear boundaries to protect our emotional well-being. This might mean limiting contact with toxic individuals, avoiding certain triggering environments, or learning to say no to unreasonable demands. By asserting our boundaries, we can create a more positive and supportive environment, reducing opportunities for unnecessary anger to arise.

Finally, seeking professional help can be beneficial for those struggling with anger issues. Therapy can provide individuals with tools and strategies to manage their anger effectively, addressing underlying issues that contribute to their emotional responses. A therapist can offer guidance, support, and coping mechanisms tailored to individual needs, fostering personal growth and healing.

In conclusion, unnecessary anger is a hidden enemy that can cause significant emotional and physical damage. It strains relationships, undermines our mental and physical health, and can be exploited by others. Understanding the nature of anger and developing strategies to manage it effectively is crucial for maintaining our well-being. By cultivating self-awareness, practicing mindfulness, improving communication skills, setting boundaries, and seeking professional help when needed, we can transform our relationship with anger and create a more positive and fulfilling life. Ultimately, learning to manage unnecessary anger empowers us to take control of our emotions, improve our relationships, and foster a healthier, happier existence.

XI

The Balance of Love and Discipline: A Parent's Guiding Principle

Parenting is one of the most profound and challenging responsibilities a person can undertake. At the heart of parenting lies love, a powerful force that drives parents to nurture, protect, and care for their children. However, loving your child does not equate to yielding to every whim or fulfilling unnecessary tantrums. This distinction is crucial, as it emphasizes the importance of instilling discipline alongside love. In this context, discipline is not merely about enforcing rules but rather about teaching valuable life skills and good habits that will serve children well into adulthood. Understanding this balance is vital, as failing to recognize it can lead to unintended consequences that may hinder a child's development.

As parents, our instinct is often to shield our children from discomfort and to fulfill their needs and desires, especially when they express dissatisfaction or anger. This instinct is natural; it stems from a deep-seated desire to see our children happy and content. However, this desire can sometimes manifest as overindulgence. When parents consistently give in to every demand or tantrum, they inadvertently teach their children that throwing fits is an effective way to get what they want. This pattern not only reinforces negative behavior but also deprives children of learning important lessons about patience, compromise, and the value of hard work.

The idea that love can blind us is a critical one. In our desire to be the "perfect" parent, we may overlook the importance of discipline in our children's lives. It's easy to fall into the trap of thinking that loving your child means always being agreeable and accommodating. However, this perspective can lead to a lack of boundaries and structure in a child's life, which are essential components for their emotional and social development. Without discipline, children may struggle to understand expectations and consequences, leading to difficulties in navigating relationships and environments outside the home.

Discipline should be viewed as a loving act rather than a punitive measure. It is essential to establish a clear set of boundaries and expectations for behavior while providing a supportive environment for children to learn and grow. This balance allows children to feel secure while also giving them the tools they need to develop self-control and responsibility. Discipline teaches children that actions have consequences, both positive and negative, and helps them understand the importance of making good choices.

One effective way to instill discipline is through consistent routines and expectations. Children thrive in environments where they know what is expected of them. Establishing a daily routine that includes responsibilities, chores, and family time can help children learn about accountability. When they understand that certain behaviors are expected, they are more likely to internalize these lessons and develop good habits.

Positive reinforcement is another crucial aspect of discipline. When children exhibit good behavior, acknowledging and rewarding it can encourage them to continue those behaviors. This could be through verbal praise, small rewards, or special privileges. Positive reinforcement not only reinforces desirable behavior but also strengthens the parent-child bond, as children feel valued and appreciated for their efforts.

Additionally, teaching discipline requires patience and understanding. Children are naturally curious and may test boundaries as a part of their development. Instead of reacting with frustration or anger, parents should approach these situations with calmness and clarity. Explaining the reasoning behind rules and expectations helps children understand the "why" behind the discipline, making them more likely to accept and follow it.

Moreover, it is crucial to model the behavior you want to see in your children. Children are keen observers and often imitate the actions and attitudes of their parents. By demonstrating self-discipline, emotional regulation, and problem-solving skills, parents can effectively teach their children to navigate challenges in a similar manner. This modeling of behavior is an invaluable lesson that will stay with children as they grow.

Another aspect to consider is the importance of emotional intelligence in the context of discipline. Teaching children to recognize and manage their emotions is a vital skill that will serve them well throughout their lives. By acknowledging their feelings, parents can help children understand that it is natural to feel upset or angry, but it is essential to express those emotions appropriately. This process fosters emotional resilience, allowing children to cope with challenges in healthier ways.

It is also important to recognize that discipline should be age-appropriate. Younger children may require more guidance and supervision, while older children and teenagers may benefit from discussions about responsibility and independence. Adapting your approach to fit your child's developmental stage ensures that discipline is effective and relevant.

As parents, we must be vigilant of the "enemy within" that can lead to overindulgence or inconsistent discipline. Love for our children is a powerful force, but it must be balanced with the responsibility of teaching life skills and values. Allowing love to overshadow the necessity of discipline can lead to unintended consequences that hinder a child's growth and development.

In conclusion, the journey of parenting is complex, filled with moments of joy and challenges alike. Love for our children is paramount, but it must be tempered with the understanding that discipline is equally important. By teaching children about boundaries, accountability, and emotional intelligence, we equip them with the skills they need to navigate the world successfully. Recognizing the need for this balance ensures that our homes are not only places of love but also nurturing environments where children can learn, grow, and flourish. As parents, it is our duty to guide our children toward a future filled with possibilities, grounded in love and reinforced by discipline.

XII

The Power of Knowledge: Understanding Its Role in Human Advancement

"Knowledge is power" is a phrase that has echoed through the ages, attributed to the philosopher Francis Bacon. This simple yet profound statement underscores the transformative potential of knowledge and education in shaping individuals and societies. Knowledge equips us with the tools necessary to navigate life's complexities, make informed decisions, and contribute meaningfully to our communities. However, the caveat that "no knowledge or half-knowledge is the enemy of humanity" emphasizes the critical importance of acquiring knowledge responsibly and comprehensively. This essay delves into the multifaceted nature of knowledge, its empowering effects, and the dangers of ignorance and incomplete understanding.

The Empowering Nature of Knowledge

Knowledge empowers individuals in various ways. Firstly, it fosters critical thinking and enhances problem-solving abilities. An educated person can analyze situations, evaluate evidence, and formulate logical conclusions. This skill is invaluable not just in personal life but also in professional settings, where the ability to assess information critically can lead to better decision-making and innovation. In an increasingly complex world, the capacity to sift through vast amounts of information and discern truth from misinformation is more crucial than ever.

Furthermore, knowledge facilitates personal growth and self-awareness. As individuals learn about diverse perspectives, cultures, and histories, they develop empathy and understanding toward others. This growth is essential for fostering harmonious relationships and communities. A well-informed individual is more likely to appreciate differences and engage in meaningful dialogue, reducing conflict and promoting collaboration.

Education also plays a vital role in economic empowerment. A well-educated workforce is fundamental to a nation's economic success. Knowledge translates into skills that drive productivity and innovation, ultimately leading to better job opportunities and higher incomes. Individuals with access to education are more likely to contribute positively to society, not just through economic participation but also by engaging in civic activities and community service.

The Dangers of Ignorance

While knowledge empowers, ignorance can have devastating consequences. Ignorance, whether willful or unintentional, can lead to poor decision-making and harmful behaviors. In personal choices, a lack of information can result in health risks, financial difficulties, or unwise life decisions. For instance, individuals who are not educated about nutrition may make poor dietary choices, leading to health problems such as obesity or diabetes. Similarly, those who lack financial literacy may fall into debt traps or fail to save for the future.

On a societal level, ignorance can fuel prejudice, discrimination, and conflict. When individuals lack knowledge about different cultures, religions, or social issues, they are more likely to hold onto stereotypes and biases. This ignorance can lead to social division and conflict, undermining the fabric of society. History has shown us that societies that fail to educate their citizens on issues of diversity, equality, and social justice often experience unrest and turmoil.

Moreover, half-knowledge—an incomplete or superficial understanding of a subject—can be particularly dangerous. It breeds misconceptions and leads to the spread of misinformation. Individuals who hold half-formed beliefs may feel emboldened to make decisions based on incomplete information, leading to actions that can harm themselves or others. In today's digital age, where information is readily available yet often unverified, the risk of spreading half-knowledge is ever-present. Social media can amplify these issues, as individuals share opinions based on limited understanding, contributing to the spread of false information.

The Responsibility of Knowledge

Given the transformative power of knowledge, it is imperative to approach education with a sense of responsibility. This responsibility lies not only with educational institutions but also with individuals, communities, and society as a whole. Lifelong learning should be embraced as a value, with the understanding that knowledge is constantly evolving. Individuals must remain curious and committed to expanding their understanding of the world.

Educational institutions play a crucial role in fostering critical thinking and a comprehensive understanding of subjects. They must go beyond rote memorization and encourage students to question, analyze, and engage with the material critically. This approach helps develop well-rounded individuals who are not only knowledgeable but also capable of applying their knowledge in practical ways.

In addition to formal education, informal learning experiences—such as discussions, workshops, and community engagement—are invaluable for broadening perspectives. Engaging with diverse groups of people and exposing oneself to different viewpoints enhances understanding and encourages empathy.

Moreover, society must prioritize access to education as a fundamental right. Ensuring that all individuals have the opportunity to pursue education, regardless of their socio-economic background, is crucial for fostering a knowledgeable and empowered citizenry. Governments, non-profits, and communities should work together to eliminate barriers to education and promote initiatives that support lifelong learning.

Conclusion

In conclusion, knowledge is indeed power, serving as a fundamental pillar for personal, social, and economic advancement. The ability to think critically, understand diverse perspectives, and make informed decisions is essential for individuals and society as a whole. Conversely, ignorance and half-knowledge can lead to poor decisions, social division, and conflict. It is crucial to approach knowledge with responsibility, fostering an environment where education is valued and lifelong learning is encouraged. By doing so, we empower ourselves and future generations to build a more informed, compassionate, and harmonious world. Embracing the pursuit of knowledge not only enhances our lives but also contributes to the betterment of humanity.

XIII

The Importance of Self-Respect: Walking Away from Those Who Take You for Granted

In a world that often demands so much from us, it is crucial to recognize the value of self-esteem and self-respect. The notion of walking away from those who take you for granted is not just a defensive maneuver; it is a powerful affirmation of your worth and a vital step toward nurturing your mental and emotional health. Our relationships should uplift us, not diminish us. When we allow others to take us for granted, we risk eroding our self-worth and compromising our sense of identity.

Self-esteem refers to the regard in which a person holds themselves; it is about recognizing your inherent value as an individual. Self-respect goes a step further, encompassing the behaviors and attitudes that reflect that self-value. Together, these qualities form a foundation upon which we build our lives, make decisions, and interact with the world. When we hold ourselves in high regard, we are more likely to engage in positive relationships, set healthy boundaries, and pursue our goals with confidence. Conversely, when we allow others to take us for granted, we send a message that our self-worth is negotiable, which can lead to feelings of inadequacy, resentment, and frustration.

Recognizing when someone takes you for granted is often not as straightforward as it may seem. It can happen in various contexts—friendships, romantic relationships, or professional settings. Common signs include feeling undervalued, unappreciated, or overlooked. You might find that your contributions go unnoticed or that your needs and feelings are consistently dismissed. Over time, these behaviors can accumulate, leading to a toxic environment where your self-esteem and self-respect are compromised.

The impact of being taken for granted can be profound. It can lead to emotional distress, anxiety, and a diminished sense of self-worth. When we consistently seek validation from others who do not appreciate us, we become trapped in a cycle of self-doubt and dependency. The more we allow this to happen, the more our self-esteem erodes, making it increasingly difficult to recognize our own value. In such scenarios, it is essential to take a step back and evaluate the dynamics of the relationship.

Walking away from those who take you for granted is an act of self-preservation. It is a powerful declaration that you value yourself enough to refuse to be treated poorly. This decision may not come easily, especially if the relationship has deep roots or significant emotional investment. However, prioritizing your mental and emotional well-being should always take precedence. Leaving behind relationships that drain your energy and undermine your self-worth opens the door to healthier connections where your value is recognized and celebrated.

Taking this step requires courage and self-awareness. It may involve confronting the reality of the situation, recognizing that you deserve better, and understanding that it is acceptable to prioritize your needs. Surrounding yourself with supportive individuals who appreciate you for who you are can enhance your self-esteem and provide the encouragement you need to thrive.

Moreover, walking away from toxic relationships is not merely about distancing yourself from negative influences; it is also about creating space for positivity in your life. This transition allows you to focus on personal growth, self-care, and self-discovery. Engaging in activities that uplift your spirit, pursuing your passions, and investing time in relationships that nurture your self-worth can lead to profound changes in your life.

As you move away from those who take you for granted, it is crucial to cultivate a healthy sense of self-worth. This involves recognizing your strengths, talents, and contributions to the world. Engage in positive self-talk and practice affirmations that reinforce your value. Surround yourself with people who appreciate and respect you, fostering an environment where your self-esteem can flourish.

Additionally, it is essential to establish and uphold healthy boundaries in your relationships. Boundaries serve as protective measures that safeguard your emotional well-being. Communicating your needs and expectations clearly can help prevent future instances of being taken for granted. It sets a precedent that you value yourself and expect others to treat you with the same regard.

Ultimately, self-esteem and self-respect are among the most valuable assets a person possesses. They are foundational to our mental and emotional health, impacting every facet of our lives—from our relationships to our careers. By walking away from those who take you for granted, you are not only preserving your self-worth but also making room for healthier, more fulfilling connections. This journey may be challenging, but it is a necessary one for reclaiming your value and fostering a life of authenticity and joy.

In conclusion, the act of walking away from relationships that undermine your self-esteem is not an act of selfishness; it is a profound act of self-love. It demonstrates a commitment to valuing yourself and prioritizing your emotional well-being. Recognizing your worth and refusing to tolerate treatment that does not reflect that worth is a powerful step toward building a life filled with respect, appreciation, and genuine connections. Embrace this journey as a path to reclaiming your self-esteem and nurturing your self-respect, allowing you to flourish in an environment that celebrates your true value.

XIV

The Hidden Threat: Identifying and Guarding Against Disguised Adversaries

In the intricate tapestry of life, where relationships and interactions form the threads of our daily experiences, it is crucial to recognize and navigate the potential threats that may arise from those closest to us. The idea that the most significant obstacles to our success and well-being can come from within our circle—relatives, friends, or individuals who outwardly present themselves as well-wishers—underline the importance of vigilance and discernment. These individuals, often cloaked in the guise of support, may harbor hidden envy and ill intentions. Understanding the characteristics of such people and learning how to identify and manage them is essential for protecting yourself and ensuring that you remain on the path to success and personal growth.

The Veiled Enemy: Recognizing the Hidden Threat

1. The Nature of Hidden Envy

Hidden envy is a subtle and often disguised emotion. Unlike overt jealousy, which can be openly expressed, hidden envy operates behind a façade of friendliness and support. Individuals who harbor hidden envy may outwardly display affection and encouragement while secretly resenting your achievements and success. Their envy is not always evident but manifests through indirect actions and behaviors that undermine your progress.

Envy can be a powerful motivator for negative behavior. When someone feels envious, their perception of your success can evoke feelings of inadequacy and frustration. These emotions can lead them to engage in actions designed to hinder your progress or diminish your achievements. Recognizing the signs of hidden envy involves paying attention to subtle cues and inconsistencies in behavior, as well as observing the overall impact of their actions on your life.

2. The Disguised Well-Wisher

Some individuals may present themselves as well-wishers but, in reality, are invested in seeing you fail. They may offer seemingly supportive advice, only for it to be counterproductive or detrimental to your goals. Their actions are often masked in the pretense of care and concern, making it challenging to discern their true intentions.

Disguised well-wishers may use various tactics to undermine your success. They might provide flawed or misleading suggestions, create obstacles, or subtly dissuade you from pursuing your goals. Their ultimate aim is to create hurdles that prevent you from achieving success or to diminish the value of your accomplishments. Identifying such individuals requires a careful evaluation of their actions and the outcomes of their advice.

3. The Impact of Success on Hidden Enemies

Success can be a double-edged sword when it comes to relationships with disguised adversaries. For those harboring hidden envy, your achievements can be perceived as a threat, triggering resentment and animosity. The more successful you become, the more pronounced their negative feelings may become, leading them to engage in behaviors designed to obstruct or diminish your success.

These individuals may attempt to sabotage your efforts by offering misleading guidance, spreading rumors, or creating unnecessary conflicts. Their goal is to interfere with your progress and to make your journey to success more difficult. Understanding the potential impact of your success on such individuals can help you anticipate and navigate their actions more effectively.

Strategies for Identifying and Managing Disguised Adversaries

1. Observe Behavioral Patterns

One of the most effective ways to identify disguised adversaries is to observe their behavioral patterns. Pay attention to how they react to your successes and the nature of their interactions with you. Look for inconsistencies between their words and actions. Genuine friends and well-wishers will celebrate your achievements and offer constructive support, whereas disguised adversaries may respond with indifference, passive-aggressive remarks, or attempts to diminish your success.

2. Assess the Impact of Their Advice

Evaluate the quality and impact of the advice or support provided by these individuals. Constructive advice is typically practical, realistic, and aimed at helping you achieve your goals. In contrast, advice from disguised adversaries may be vague, impractical, or intentionally misleading. If you notice that their suggestions consistently lead to negative outcomes or obstacles, it may be a sign that their intentions are not as benign as they appear.

3. Monitor the Dynamics of Your Interactions

Pay attention to the dynamics of your interactions with these individuals. Disguised adversaries often use subtle tactics to undermine your confidence and progress. They may engage in passive-aggressive behavior, criticize your efforts indirectly, or create situations that cause unnecessary stress. By monitoring these dynamics, you can gain insights into their true intentions and adjust your approach accordingly.

4. Set Boundaries and Protect Your Goals

Establishing clear boundaries is essential for protecting yourself from disguised adversaries. Communicate your expectations and limits assertively, and be mindful of the influence these individuals have on your decision-making process. Guard your personal and professional goals by limiting the extent to which you share sensitive information or seek advice from those who have demonstrated dubious intentions.

5. Seek External Perspectives

Consult with trusted mentors, colleagues, or friends who have no vested interest in your success. External perspectives can provide valuable insights and help you gain a more objective view of your interactions with disguised adversaries. They can offer guidance on how to navigate challenging situations and provide support in maintaining focus on your goals.

6. Focus on Self-Awareness and Resilience

Cultivating self-awareness and resilience is crucial for managing the impact of disguised adversaries. Recognize your own strengths, values, and goals, and remain focused on your path to success. Develop coping strategies to handle setbacks and maintain your confidence in the face of adversity. Building resilience will help you navigate challenges and stay true to your objectives despite the presence of hidden threats.

Conclusion: Navigating the Complex Terrain of Relationships

The presence of disguised adversaries within your circle—whether relatives, friends, or acquaintances—presents a significant challenge. These individuals, who may appear to be well-wishers, often harbor hidden envy and seek to undermine your success. By recognizing the characteristics of such people and implementing strategies to manage their influence, you can protect your self-esteem and progress effectively.

Understanding the nature of hidden envy, identifying disguised well-wishers, and assessing the impact of their actions are key steps in navigating these complex relationships. Observing behavioral patterns, evaluating advice, setting boundaries, and seeking external perspectives can help you maintain focus and resilience. Ultimately, the ability to identify and guard against these hidden threats will empower you to achieve your goals and foster positive, supportive relationships.

In the intricate dance of personal and professional life, remaining vigilant and discerning will ensure that you surround yourself with individuals who genuinely support and uplift you, rather than those who seek to hinder your success. By protecting your self-esteem and navigating these challenges with care, you can continue to pursue your ambitions and build a fulfilling and prosperous future.

XV

Unmasking the Hidden Enemy: The Veil over Our Eyes

In the journey of life, we often face adversaries that threaten our progress and well-being. These enemies can take many forms—external challenges, negative influences, or even toxic relationships. However, the most insidious enemy of all is not external; it dwells within us, obscuring our perception of reality and hindering our growth. This enemy resides on the "eye cover," a metaphorical veil that limits our vision and prevents us from seeing things as they truly are. Understanding and overcoming this internal adversary is crucial for personal development and achieving our goals.

The Nature of the Internal Enemy

Our internal enemy manifests in various ways: self-doubt, fear, ignorance, and complacency. It thrives on our insecurities, feeding off our negative thoughts and experiences. Often, we are unaware of its presence, allowing it to manipulate our beliefs and actions. This internal adversary influences our decisions, shapes our perceptions, and can even sabotage our aspirations. The enemy lurking behind our "eye cover" obscures the truth, making it challenging to recognize opportunities, acknowledge our potential, and confront our weaknesses.

The Veil of Perception

The "eye cover" symbolizes our limited understanding and preconceived notions. Just as physical blindness restricts our ability to navigate the world, this metaphorical blindness prevents us from recognizing the reality around us. We may become so entrenched in our beliefs that we fail to see alternative perspectives or truths. This narrow view can lead to a distorted sense of self, where we underestimate our capabilities or overestimate our limitations.

The veil can also manifest through cognitive biases—mental shortcuts that skew our judgment. Confirmation bias, for example, causes us to seek information that reinforces our existing beliefs while dismissing contradictory evidence. Similarly, the halo effect can lead us to judge a person's entire character based on a single positive attribute, thus obscuring the whole truth. These biases cloud our judgment and distort our perceptions, allowing our internal enemy to thrive unchecked.

Identifying the Enemy Within

To combat this internal adversary, we must first recognize its presence. Self-awareness is the key to unveiling the truths hidden beneath our eye cover. Reflecting on our thoughts, emotions, and behaviors can help us identify patterns that reveal our internal enemy. Journaling, meditation, or engaging in honest conversations with trusted friends or mentors can provide valuable insights into our inner workings.

Once we identify our internal enemy, we can begin to challenge the narratives it has constructed. This involves questioning our beliefs and confronting the fears that limit us. Are the stories we tell ourselves based on reality, or are they mere fabrications of our insecurities? By seeking evidence to support or refute these beliefs, we can gain a clearer understanding of our true capabilities.

Replacing the Veil with Clarity

Once we have acknowledged the presence of our internal enemy, the next step is to work towards replacing the veil of perception with clarity. This involves cultivating a mindset of openness and curiosity. Embracing new experiences, seeking diverse perspectives, and remaining receptive to feedback can help expand our understanding of the world and ourselves.

Mindfulness practices can also play a significant role in this process. By training ourselves to remain present and aware of our thoughts and emotions, we can create space for reflection and growth. Mindfulness allows us to observe our internal narratives without judgment, enabling us to break free from their grip and choose more empowering thoughts.

The Journey to Overcoming the Internal Enemy

Overcoming our internal enemy is not a one-time event but a continuous journey. It requires dedication and resilience as we navigate the challenges and setbacks along the way. We must be patient with ourselves, recognizing that transformation takes time and effort. Embracing failure as a learning opportunity rather than a definitive endpoint can help us build resilience and foster a growth mindset.

In this journey, it is essential to surround ourselves with supportive individuals who encourage our growth and challenge our limiting beliefs. Constructive criticism and honest feedback from trusted friends and mentors can help us remain accountable and gain new insights into our blind spots. Building a community that fosters open dialogue and encourages exploration can create an environment conducive to personal growth.

Embracing the Reality

Ultimately, the goal of this journey is to embrace reality—the truth about ourselves, our capabilities, and the world around us. When we remove the veil obscuring our vision, we gain the power to make informed decisions and pursue our aspirations with clarity and conviction. By winning over the internal enemy, we unlock our potential and take control of our lives.

In conclusion, the most formidable enemy is often the one that resides within us, hiding behind a veil that limits our perception. By recognizing and confronting this adversary, we can gain clarity and insight into our true selves. The journey to overcoming this internal enemy is one of self-discovery, resilience, and growth. As we strive to unmask our hidden adversaries and replace the veil over our eyes with clarity, we empower ourselves to navigate the complexities of life with confidence and authenticity.

XVI

The Power of Action: Living the Words We Speak

In a world where communication flows seamlessly through countless channels, the importance of authenticity has never been greater. We often hear the phrase, "Practice what you preach," a call to align our actions with our words. This principle transcends mere rhetoric; it is a foundational element of integrity, credibility, and personal growth. Words, while powerful in their own right, hold little value if not backed by genuine action. This exploration will delve into the significance of this statement, emphasizing the necessity of living our values and beliefs through our actions.

Understanding the Concept

At its core, "practice what you preach" highlights the discrepancy that can exist between what individuals say and what they do. It speaks to the idea that our beliefs and values should inform our behaviors and choices. When our actions align with our words, we build trust with ourselves and others. This alignment fosters respect, credibility, and a sense of authenticity, while a disconnect can lead to skepticism, disillusionment, and a loss of integrity.

For instance, a leader who advocates for transparency but operates behind closed doors may create an atmosphere of distrust among their team. Similarly, a mentor who encourages others to pursue their passions but fails to take steps toward their own goals may inadvertently undermine their credibility. In both cases, the absence of action diminishes the value of the spoken words, highlighting the necessity of embodying the principles we espouse.

The Importance of Integrity

Integrity is often described as the adherence to moral and ethical principles. Practicing what we preach is a manifestation of integrity, as it demands that we hold ourselves accountable to the standards we set for others. When we demonstrate consistency between our beliefs and our actions, we cultivate a strong sense of self-respect and personal integrity.

This alignment is particularly important in leadership roles. Leaders who model the behaviors they expect from their teams foster an environment of trust and accountability. When employees see their leaders actively demonstrating the values of the organization—such as respect, collaboration, and innovation—they are more likely to emulate those behaviors themselves. This creates a positive feedback loop that strengthens the organizational culture and drives collective success.

The Ripple Effect of Actions

Actions have a profound ripple effect that extends beyond the individual. When we practice what we preach, we inspire others to do the same. Our behavior serves as a powerful example, influencing those around us to align their actions with their values. This can create a culture of accountability and authenticity, where individuals feel empowered to express their beliefs through their actions.

Consider a community activist who advocates for environmental sustainability. By adopting eco-friendly practices in their personal life—such as reducing waste, using renewable energy, and promoting local resources—they not only reinforce their message but also encourage others to follow suit. The activist's actions can spark a movement, inspiring individuals to reevaluate their habits and make positive changes in their lives. This chain reaction illustrates the profound impact that aligning words and actions can have on a broader scale.

The Personal Journey of Alignment

The journey of aligning our actions with our words is deeply personal and often challenging. It requires self-reflection and a willingness to confront the discrepancies in our lives. To truly practice what we preach, we must examine our beliefs, values, and motivations. Are we living in accordance with the principles we espouse? Are there areas where our actions do not align with our stated beliefs?

This process may involve making difficult choices and sacrifices. For instance, someone who advocates for work-life balance but consistently prioritizes work over personal well-being may need to reevaluate their priorities. Embracing the challenge of aligning our actions with our words can lead to profound personal growth and fulfillment. It encourages us to live authentically and with intention, cultivating a deeper sense of purpose.

The Dangers of Illegitimacy

Conversely, failing to practice what we preach can have detrimental consequences. Illegitimacy erodes trust, both within us and in our relationships with others. When our actions do not reflect our words, we create a dissonance that can lead to feelings of guilt, shame, and dissatisfaction. This internal conflict can hinder our ability to engage meaningfully with the world around us.

Moreover, when others perceive us as inauthentic, it can lead to a loss of credibility. People are naturally drawn to individuals who embody their beliefs and values, and when we fail to live up to our stated principles, we risk alienating those who may have otherwise supported or followed us. The loss of trust can be particularly damaging in professional settings, where collaboration and teamwork rely on mutual respect and integrity.

Conclusion: The Call to Action

In conclusion, the adage "practice what you preach" serves as a powerful reminder of the necessity of aligning our actions with our words. Authenticity, integrity, and the ripple effect of our behaviors underscore the importance of living out our values in a tangible way. While words can inspire, they hold little value if not backed by action.

As individuals, we are called to reflect on our beliefs and examine the ways in which our actions align with those beliefs. This journey may require introspection, difficult choices, and a commitment to personal growth. Ultimately, the effort to practice what we preach enriches not only our own lives but also the lives of those around us, fostering a culture of authenticity, trust, and collective progress.

Living our values through action is not just a personal endeavor; it is a powerful testament to our character and a catalyst for positive change in our communities. So let us rise to the challenge, embrace our principles, and take meaningful action that reflects the words we speak.

XVII

Understanding Your Adversaries: The Importance of Knowing Your Foe

L ife often presents itself as a series of challenges and adversities that can feel overwhelmingly harsh. Each day brings a new set of trials, whether they stem from personal relationships, professional environments, or the unpredictability of circumstances. However, navigating this harsh reality becomes significantly easier when one possesses awareness and understanding—especially about those who may act as obstacles on our journey. This brings us to the essential wisdom encapsulated in the phrase, "Know your foe." Understanding your adversaries—be they individuals, circumstances, or even your inner self—can be a powerful tool in managing life's challenges effectively.

The Nature of Adversity

Adversity is an inherent part of the human experience. It can arise in various forms, from the struggles of daily life to significant setbacks that test our resilience. While some challenges are external—such as difficult relationships, unsupportive colleagues, or systemic obstacles—others are internal, manifesting as self-doubt, fear, or unresolved trauma. Understanding the multifaceted nature of adversity is crucial; it allows us to confront not only the external challenges we face but also the internal battles that can hinder our progress.

Recognizing that life can be harsh is the first step toward building resilience. Acceptance of reality is empowering; it shifts the focus from wishing for an easier path to developing the skills and mindset needed to navigate difficulties. However, this journey is not just about individual resilience; it also involves understanding the dynamics of our relationships and the people who may influence our lives, positively or negatively.

The Role of Awareness

Awareness is a powerful ally in combating the adversities of life. It encompasses not only self-awareness but also social awareness— the understanding of those around us, their motivations, and their potential impact on our lives. This awareness enables us to identify who our allies are and who may pose as obstacles. Knowing your foe means understanding their intentions, behaviors, and the hidden dynamics that may affect your journey.

In personal relationships, for example, being aware of individuals who harbor hidden envy or resentment can help you navigate interactions more wisely. Such individuals may present themselves as friends but, in reality, may undermine your efforts or celebrate your failures. Recognizing these traits early allows you to set boundaries and protect your emotional well-being. This proactive approach not only safeguards your self-esteem but also enhances your ability to foster genuine relationships with those who genuinely support your growth.

The Importance of Knowing Your Foe

The concept of knowing your foe extends beyond interpersonal relationships; it also applies to understanding systemic challenges and personal limitations. In a professional context, for instance, knowing your competitors—be they individuals vying for the same position, market forces, or organizational structures—can equip you with strategies to excel. Awareness of the competitive landscape helps in identifying opportunities and threats, allowing for informed decision-making that can lead to success.

Furthermore, understanding your own limitations—your fears, insecurities, and areas of weakness—is equally important. Recognizing these internal foes empowers you to develop coping strategies, seek support, and pursue personal growth. It allows you to approach challenges with a more balanced perspective, acknowledging that failure and setbacks are often integral components of success. By understanding and confronting these internal adversaries, you can cultivate resilience and adaptability.

Strategies for Knowing Your Foe

1. **Self-Reflection:** Regular self-reflection is essential for understanding your own motivations, fears, and limitations. Journaling, meditation, or engaging in deep conversations with trusted friends can provide valuable insights into your inner self. This understanding allows you to recognize when your internal adversaries are holding you back.

2. **Observation:** Pay close attention to the behaviors and motivations of those around you. Observe how people react to your successes and failures. Look for patterns that may indicate hidden envy or resentment. This observation can help you discern who genuinely supports you and who may act as a foe in disguise.

3. **Seek Feedback:** Engaging with trusted friends, mentors, or colleagues can provide external perspectives on your interactions and challenges. Constructive feedback can illuminate blind spots and help you better understand the dynamics at play in your relationships and professional life.

4. **Set Boundaries:** Once you identify individuals who may undermine your efforts or emotional well-being, establish clear boundaries.

Protecting your space from negativity is crucial for maintaining focus and nurturing your self-esteem.

5. **Continuous Learning**: Stay informed and educated about your field, personal development, and emotional intelligence. This knowledge equips you with the tools to navigate challenges effectively and make informed decisions about the relationships you cultivate.

Embracing Resilience

The journey of life is undoubtedly filled with obstacles, but it is also a path of growth and opportunity. By embracing resilience and cultivating awareness—especially regarding those who may act as foes—we empower ourselves to navigate the harsh realities of existence more effectively. The phrase "Know your foe" serves as a reminder that understanding our adversaries, both internal and external, is vital for personal and professional success.

In conclusion, life may be harsh, but it becomes manageable when armed with the knowledge of oneself and others. Recognizing the nature of adversity, fostering awareness, and employing strategies to identify and mitigate the impact of foes can significantly enhance our ability to thrive. Ultimately, knowing your foe is about equipping yourself with the tools necessary to confront challenges head-on and emerge stronger, wiser, and more resilient in the face of life's complexities.

XVIII

The Art of Intellectual Decision-Making: Navigating Choices with Clarity

Decision-making is an intrinsic part of the human experience, shaping our lives in profound ways. While emotions are a natural and important aspect of our decision-making process, relying solely on them can lead to choices that may not serve our best interests. Intellectual decision-making, on the other hand, emphasizes reason, analysis, and objective assessment, ultimately leading to more informed and effective outcomes. This essay explores the necessity of intellectual decision-making, its benefits, and strategies to cultivate this essential skill.

Understanding Decision-Making

At its core, decision-making involves evaluating options and choosing a course of action. This process can be influenced by various factors, including personal values, past experiences, and emotional responses. Emotions can provide valuable insights; they often guide us toward what feels right or wrong. However, they can also cloud our judgment, leading us to make hasty or irrational choices. For instance, decisions made in the heat of anger or frustration may not reflect our true desires or best interests, resulting in regret or unintended consequences.

Conversely, intellectual decision-making promotes a balanced approach that prioritizes rational thinking over impulsive reactions. By engaging our cognitive faculties, we can analyze situations, weigh pros and cons, and anticipate the potential outcomes of our choices. This intellectual rigor can help us avoid the pitfalls of emotional decision-making and foster a clearer understanding of our objectives.

The Benefits of Intellectual Decision-Making

1. **Clarity and Focus:** Intellectual decision-making encourages clarity of thought. By systematically evaluating options, we can identify what truly matters to us and eliminate distractions or irrelevant factors. This focused approach leads to more coherent decisions that align with our long-term goals.

2. **Reduced Risk of Regret:** Emotions can lead us to make impulsive decisions that we may later regret. By taking the time to think critically and analytically, we can minimize the likelihood of making choices we will later wish to reverse. This foresight is crucial in both personal and professional contexts, where decisions can have lasting repercussions.

3. **Enhanced Problem-Solving Skills:** Engaging in intellectual decision-making fosters better problem-solving abilities. It encourages us to break down complex issues into manageable parts, allowing us to tackle challenges systematically. This skill is invaluable in a world that often presents multifaceted problems requiring innovative solutions.

4. **Informed Choices:** Intellectual decision-making relies on data and evidence. By gathering information and considering various perspectives, we can make choices grounded in reality rather than subjective feelings. This informed approach increases our confidence in the decisions we make, reducing uncertainty and doubt.

5. **Long-Term Perspective:** Emotional responses are often rooted in immediate circumstances, leading to short-term thinking. In contrast, intellectual decision-making encourages us to consider the long-term implications of our choices. This broader perspective helps us make decisions that align with our overarching goals and values.

Strategies for Cultivating Intellectual Decision-Making

1. **Pause and Reflect:** Before making a decision, take a moment to pause and reflect. This simple act can help you create space between your emotions and your choices. Consider what is driving your emotional response and whether it is relevant to the decision at hand.

2. **Gather Information:** Effective decision-making relies on accurate information. Research your options thoroughly, considering various sources and perspectives. This not only enhances your understanding but also enables you to make choices based on facts rather than feelings.

3. **List Pros and Cons:** Creating a pros and cons list can clarify your options. This visual representation of the potential benefits and drawbacks of each choice allows you to weigh them objectively. It also helps you identify any biases or emotional influences affecting your judgment.

4. **Seek External Perspectives:** Engaging with trusted friends, colleagues, or mentors can provide valuable insights. Others may see aspects of a situation that you might overlook, helping you to broaden your perspective. Their feedback can also challenge your assumptions and encourage more critical thinking.

5. **Practice Mindfulness:** Mindfulness techniques can help you become more aware of your emotional responses and thought

patterns. By cultivating mindfulness, you can develop greater emotional regulation, allowing you to respond to situations with clarity and purpose rather than impulse.

6. **Embrace Failure as a Learning Opportunity:** Understand that not every decision will lead to the desired outcome. Instead of fearing failure, view it as a chance to learn and grow. Analyzing past decisions can provide valuable insights that inform future choices, enhancing your decision-making skills over time.

Conclusion

In an increasingly complex world, the ability to make informed, rational decisions is more important than ever. While emotions play a vital role in our lives, they should not dictate our choices. By embracing intellectual decision-making, we can navigate our lives with clarity, confidence, and purpose. The journey to becoming a more effective decision-maker requires practice, self-reflection, and a commitment to lifelong learning. Ultimately, the art of intellectual decision-making empowers us to shape our lives in alignment with our values and aspirations, steering us toward a future defined by thoughtful and deliberate choices.

XIX

The Pursuit of Long-Term Goals: Balancing Immediate Gratification and Future Success

In today's fast-paced world, the allure of instant gratification is ever-present. Whether it's the convenience of fast food, the ease of online shopping, or the dopamine rush from social media notifications, many individuals find themselves caught in a cycle of seeking short-term happiness. While these quick fixes can provide temporary satisfaction, they often come at the expense of long-term goals and aspirations. The challenge lies in navigating this delicate balance, making conscious choices that align with our deeper objectives and values. This essay explores the implications of prioritizing long-term goals over short-term pleasures, the psychological underpinnings of our choices, and practical strategies for cultivating a mindset geared toward sustainable fulfillment.

Understanding the Allure of Short-Term Happiness

Human beings are inherently wired to seek pleasure and avoid pain. This biological impulse has served us well throughout evolution, helping us navigate an unpredictable environment. However, in modern society, this instinct often manifests as a preference for immediate rewards over delayed gratification. Short-term happiness can feel more tangible and achievable than the long, often arduous path to long-term success.

For instance, consider the case of a young professional who receives a substantial bonus at work. The temptation to spend that bonus on a luxury vacation or a new gadget can overshadow the more prudent option of saving or investing the money for future financial stability. The immediate joy of indulgence may seem more appealing than the abstract promise of a secure future.

This mindset can lead to a pattern of decision-making that prioritizes fleeting pleasures, ultimately jeopardizing long-term goals such as career advancement, financial independence, and personal growth.

The Consequences of Prioritizing Short-Term Gratification

1. **Financial Instability:** One of the most significant areas affected by prioritizing short-term happiness is personal finance. Impulsive spending on luxuries or experiences can drain savings and lead to debt. This financial instability can create stress and anxiety, undermining the very happiness these short-term pleasures were meant to provide.

2. **Health Implications:** In the pursuit of immediate gratification, individuals may neglect their health. For example, choosing convenience foods over nutritious meals or skipping exercise for a night of binge-watching can have detrimental effects on physical and mental well-being. Over time, these choices can lead to serious health issues that compromise long-term quality of life.

3. **Career Setbacks:** In a professional context, the temptation to take shortcuts for immediate rewards can hinder career advancement. Relying on quick wins rather than investing in skill development and networking can create a stagnant career trajectory. Long-term success often requires hard work, perseverance, and a willingness to make sacrifices in the present for future rewards.

4. **Damaged Relationships:** Short-term gratification can also impact personal relationships. Prioritizing immediate pleasures over meaningful connections—such as choosing to socialize at bars instead of nurturing friendships—can lead to isolation and dissatisfaction. Strong, supportive relationships are built over time and require effort and commitment.

The Psychology of Delayed Gratification

Understanding the psychological mechanisms behind delayed gratification is crucial for fostering a mindset oriented toward long-term goals. The concept of delayed gratification, popularized by the famous Marshmallow Experiment conducted by psychologist Walter Mischel in the 1960s, illustrates this idea. In the experiment, children were given the choice between one immediate rewards (a marshmallow) or two rewards if they waited for a short period. The ability to wait for the second marshmallow was correlated with better life outcomes in various areas, including academic performance, health, and financial stability.

This finding underscores the importance of self-control and the ability to envision future rewards. Those who can resist immediate temptations often reap the benefits later in life. Developing self-discipline is key to achieving long-term goals, and it begins with recognizing that the decisions we make today can significantly impact our futures.

Strategies for Prioritizing Long-Term Goals

1. **Set Clear, Achievable Goals:** Begin by defining your long-term objectives. Whether they pertain to your career, health, or personal relationships, having clear goals provides direction and motivation. Break these goals down into smaller, actionable steps to make them more manageable and attainable.

2. **Create a Reward System:** To combat the allure of short-term gratification, establish a reward system that aligns with your long-term goals. For example, if saving money for a major purchase, treat yourself to a smaller, inexpensive reward when you hit savings milestones. This approach can provide motivation without jeopardizing your overall objective.

3. **Practice Mindfulness:** Mindfulness techniques can help you become more aware of your impulses and thought patterns. By cultivating present-moment awareness, you can better assess whether your choices align with your long-term goals. Take a moment to pause and reflect before making decisions, especially those driven by immediate desires.

4. **Visualize Future Success:** Visualization is a powerful tool for reinforcing long-term goals. Spend time imagining the benefits of achieving your objectives and how they will enhance your life. This mental imagery can create a sense of urgency to pursue your goals, making the sacrifices for immediate gratification feel more worthwhile.

5. **Surround Yourself with Supportive People:** Engage with individuals who share similar aspirations and values. A supportive community can provide encouragement and accountability, making it easier to resist short-term temptations. Sharing your long-term goals with others can also create a sense of commitment and motivation.

Conclusion

In a world dominated by the pursuit of instant gratification, it is essential to recognize the importance of long-term goals. The choices we make today can significantly impact our futures, and sacrificing these aspirations for fleeting pleasures often leads to regret and dissatisfaction. By cultivating self-discipline, setting clear goals, and adopting a mindful approach to decision-making, we can navigate the complexities of life with purpose and intention. Ultimately, the path to true fulfillment lies in balancing short-term happiness with the pursuit of our long-term aspirations, creating a life that is both satisfying and meaningful.

XX

The Everlasting Bonds: Respecting Our Parents through All Stages of Life

Life is an ever-evolving journey filled with transitions, experiences, and relationships. As we navigate through various stages, one truth remains constant: the unconditional love and support of our parents. In a world that is continually changing—marked by shifting societal norms, technological advancements, and personal ambitions—our parents often stand as a stable foundation. They are the individuals who have nurtured us, instilled values in us, and shaped our identities. This essay explores the significance of respecting our parents throughout their lives, acknowledging their sacrifices, and recognizing the profound impact of our relationships with them.

The Unchanging Nature of Parental Love

From the moment of our birth, our parents become our first caregivers, protectors, and teachers. Their love is often described as unconditional—a bond that transcends time and circumstance. Unlike many relationships that may fade or evolve, the connection we share with our parents is uniquely enduring. They witness our growth from infancy to adulthood, experiencing our triumphs and challenges alongside us.

As we progress through life, we inevitably encounter change: friendships may dissolve, romantic relationships may end, and career paths may shift. However, our parents remain steadfast. They provide a sense of continuity amidst the chaos of life. This unwavering presence deserves recognition and respect, especially as they age and navigate their own challenges.

Acknowledging Their Sacrifices

Every parent makes sacrifices—some seen, some unseen. They dedicate their time, resources, and energy to ensure our well-being and success. Whether it's working long hours to provide for the family, forgoing personal desires for our benefit, or being emotionally available during our difficult times, their sacrifices often go unnoticed.

As we grow older, it is vital to reflect on these contributions and express gratitude. Simple gestures—such as thanking them for their support, acknowledging their hard work, or spending quality time together—can go a long way in reinforcing our respect for them. Understanding their sacrifices allows us to appreciate the depth of their commitment and the love they have invested in our lives.

The Impact of Aging on Relationships

As parents age, their needs and challenges evolve. They may face health issues, emotional struggles, or the loss of friends and family members. This transition can be difficult for them and may create a role reversal where children become caregivers. It's essential to approach this stage with empathy and respect.

Supporting aging parents requires patience and understanding. They may not always adapt to change as easily as we do. Their preferences, beliefs, and habits, shaped by decades of experience, may differ from the contemporary values we embrace. During these times, it is crucial to listen to their concerns and respect their choices, even when we may not fully understand them.

Building a Respectful Relationship

Respecting our parents at every stage of their lives involves active engagement in the relationship. Here are several ways to cultivate this respect:

1. **Open Communication:** Establishing a dialogue with our parents can foster mutual understanding. Share your thoughts and feelings, and encourage them to express theirs. Listening actively shows that you value their opinions and experiences, which strengthens the bond between you.

2. **Quality Time:** In our busy lives, it can be easy to overlook spending time with our parents. Prioritize regular visits, phone calls, or shared activities. These moments reinforce your connection and allow you to create lasting memories together.

3. **Acknowledge Their Wisdom:** Parents possess a wealth of knowledge and experience. Seek their advice when facing challenges or making significant decisions. Recognizing their wisdom not only demonstrates respect but also affirms their role as guides in your life.

4. **Support Their Independence:** As parent's age, they may struggle with their independence. Encourage them to engage in activities that promote their well-being, whether it's pursuing hobbies, maintaining social connections, or making their own decisions. Supporting their independence fosters respect and affirms their dignity.

5. **Express Gratitude:** Regularly express your appreciation for their efforts, both past and present. A heartfelt thank-you can remind them of their significance in your life and reinforce the bond of respect and love.

The Cycle of Life and Parental Care

As the saying goes, "what goes around comes around." The cycle of life means that as we age, we will also face similar challenges that our parents have navigated. Caring for aging parents often mirrors the care they provided to us as children. This role reversal emphasizes the importance of empathy and understanding as we support them in their later years.

Moreover, caring for our parents can be an opportunity for personal growth. It teaches us patience, compassion, and resilience—qualities that are invaluable as we navigate our own lives. By honoring our parents during this phase, we not only respect their legacy but also enrich our own lives.

Conclusion

In a world characterized by constant change, our parents remain a fundamental part of our lives—a source of love, wisdom, and stability. Respecting them at every stage of their lives is not just an obligation; it is an acknowledgment of the profound impact they have had on our personal journeys. By recognizing their sacrifices, engaging in open communication, and supporting their needs as they age, we can cultivate a relationship built on mutual respect and understanding.

Ultimately, the bond between parents and children is a lifelong connection that transcends time. By honoring and respecting our parents, we ensure that this relationship remains strong and meaningful, enriching both our lives and theirs. As we navigate the complexities of life, let us remember the enduring love of our parents and commit to honoring them at every age, appreciating the irreplaceable role they play in shaping who we are.

XXI

Staying Grounded: The Importance of Maintaining Your Roots in a Changing World

In an ever-evolving society filled with challenges and distractions, the pursuit of success often leads individuals away from their foundational values and principles. As we navigate our personal and professional journeys, the temptation to chase fleeting trends, societal expectations, or material gains can become overwhelming. However, staying grounded and remaining true to our roots is essential for achieving lasting success and fulfillment. This essay explores the significance of maintaining one's roots, the internal conflicts that can arise, and practical strategies to ensure we stay connected to our core values throughout our lives.

Understanding the Concept of Roots

Roots are the foundational beliefs, values, and experiences that shape who we are. They often stem from our upbringing, cultural heritage, and personal experiences. These roots provide us with a sense of identity, guiding our decisions and actions as we navigate the complexities of life. When we stay connected to our roots, we are more likely to align our choices with our true selves, fostering authenticity and integrity.

Conversely, losing sight of our roots can lead to confusion and disconnection. In the pursuit of success—whether defined by wealth, status, or societal approval—we may find ourselves compromising our values or succumbing to external pressures. This divergence can create an internal conflict, often referred to as the "enemy within," which manifests as self-doubt, anxiety, and a sense of unfullfillment.

The Enemy Within: Internal Conflicts

The "enemy within" is the voice of doubt, fear, and temptation that can divert us from our true paths. This internal adversary can take many forms, including:

1. **Self-Doubt:** As we strive for success, we may encounter self-doubt that questions our abilities, worthiness, and potential. This voice can lead us to abandon our roots, convincing us that we need to conform to others' expectations or follow trends that do not resonate with our core values.

2. **Fear of Failure:** The fear of failing can paralyze us and deter us from pursuing our passions. This fear may compel us to make choices that are safe but not authentic, leading us further away from our roots and closer to a life dictated by others.

3. **Comparison to Others:** In a world dominated by social media and constant connectivity, it is easy to fall into the trap of comparing ourselves to others. This comparison can amplify feelings of inadequacy and pressure us to abandon our roots in favor of a more superficial path to success.

4. **Desire for Approval:** The desire for validation from others can drive us to make choices that conflict with our values. Seeking external approval often leads us to prioritize others' opinions over our own, resulting in a disconnection from our true selves.

The Importance of Staying Grounded

Maintaining a connection to our roots is essential for several reasons:

1. **Authenticity:** Staying grounded allows us to live authentically, aligning our actions with our values. When we embrace our roots, we are more likely to pursue paths that resonate with our true selves, fostering a sense of fulfillment and purpose.

2. **Resilience**: In times of adversity, our roots can serve as a source of strength. When faced with challenges, returning to our core values can provide clarity and guidance, helping us navigate obstacles with resilience and determination.

3. **Sustained Success:** Success that is not aligned with our values is often short-lived. By staying connected to our roots, we can achieve success that is not only meaningful but also sustainable. This alignment ensures that our achievements resonate with our true selves, leading to long-term fulfillment.

4. **Meaningful Relationships:** Staying true to our roots fosters genuine connections with others. When we embrace our values, we attract individuals who share similar beliefs and aspirations, creating a supportive community that reinforces our commitment to our roots.

Strategies for Staying Connected to Your Roots

1. **Reflect on Your Values**: Take time to identify and articulate your core values. What principles guide your decisions and actions? Reflecting on these values can help you stay grounded as you navigate challenges and opportunities.

2. **Set Intentional Goals:** When pursuing success, ensure that your goals align with your values. Set intentions that reflect your true aspirations rather than external pressures or societal expectations.

This alignment will help you remain connected to your roots throughout your journey.

3. **Practice Mindfulness:** Mindfulness techniques can enhance your self-awareness and help you recognize when you are drifting away from your roots. Engaging in regular mindfulness practices, such as meditation or journaling, allows you to reflect on your thoughts and feelings, reinforcing your connection to your core values.

4. **Seek Support:** Surround yourself with individuals who share your values and beliefs. Building a supportive community can provide encouragement and accountability, helping you stay grounded in your pursuits. Share your aspirations and challenges with trusted friends or mentors who understand your journey.

5. **Embrace Your Heritage:** Your cultural heritage and upbringing are integral aspects of your roots. Embrace and celebrate your heritage by participating in traditions, customs, and practices that resonate with you. This connection can strengthen your identity and remind you of your foundational values.

6. **Learn from Challenges:** View challenges and setbacks as opportunities for growth. Reflect on how these experiences relate to your roots and values. By learning from adversity, you can reinforce your commitment to staying true to yourself.

Conclusion

In a world filled with distractions and pressures to conform, the importance of staying connected to our roots cannot be overstated. The "enemy within" may try to divert us from our foundational values, leading to confusion and discontent. However, by prioritizing authenticity, resilience, and sustained success, we can navigate our journeys with purpose and integrity.

Staying grounded is not merely about achieving success; it is about living a life that is meaningful and true to ourselves. By reflecting on our values, setting intentional goals, and surrounding ourselves with supportive individuals, we can ensure that we remain connected to our roots, regardless of the changes that life may bring. Ultimately, embracing our roots empowers us to face challenges with confidence, cultivate meaningful relationships, and pursue a path that resonates with our true selves. In doing so, we create a life filled with lasting fulfillment and genuine success.

XXII

The Courage to Question: Overcoming Fear to Seek Truth

In a world filled with complexities and uncertainties, the ability to ask questions is one of the most powerful tools we possess. Questions drive discovery, foster understanding, and promote change. Yet, despite the significance of inquiry, many people hesitate to voice their concerns, fearing the repercussions of their questions or the discomfort they might cause. This essay explores the importance of asking questions, the barriers created by fear, and strategies for fostering a culture of inquiry and open dialogue.

The Importance of Asking Questions

Questions serve as the foundation for knowledge. They allow us to explore, investigate, and challenge the status quo. Whether in personal relationships, professional environments, or broader societal contexts, asking questions can lead to greater clarity, deeper understanding, and meaningful change. Here are several reasons why asking questions is crucial:

1. **Promotes Critical Thinking:** Questions encourage critical thinking by prompting us to analyze information rather than accept it at face value. By questioning assumptions, we develop a more nuanced understanding of the world around us.

2. **Encourages Growth and Learning:** The act of questioning is fundamental to learning. By seeking answers, we expand our

knowledge base and gain new perspectives, enabling personal and intellectual growth.

3. **Fosters Accountability:** In various contexts—be it in the workplace, government, or social issues—asking questions holds individuals and institutions accountable. It ensures that actions and decisions are scrutinized, promoting transparency and ethical behavior.

4. **Drives Innovation:** Inquiry is the catalyst for innovation. By questioning existing practices and exploring new possibilities, we can uncover creative solutions to complex problems.

5. **Strengthens Relationships:** In personal relationships, asking questions can deepen connections. It demonstrates a genuine interest in others' thoughts and feelings, fostering open communication and trust.

The Barrier of Fear

Despite the clear benefits of questioning, fear often serves as a significant barrier to inquiry. This fear can manifest in various forms, including:

1. **Fear of Repercussions:** Individuals may fear backlash or negative consequences for speaking out or asking difficult questions, especially in hierarchical structures like workplaces or institutions. This fear can stifle honest dialogue and perpetuate a culture of silence.

2. **Fear of Judgment:** The fear of being judged or ridiculed can deter individuals from expressing their concerns or uncertainties. This self-consciousness can lead to a reluctance to ask questions, even when they are necessary for clarity and understanding.

3. **Fear of the Unknown:** Questions often lead to uncertainty, and many people prefer the comfort of known boundaries.

The fear of what might be uncovered can prevent individuals from asking questions that could reveal uncomfortable truths or challenge long-held beliefs.

4. **Fear of Change:** Inquiry often leads to change, and for many, change is intimidating. The fear of disrupting the status quo can deter individuals from questioning existing practices or norms, even when they are harmful or outdated.

Overcoming Fear to Foster Inquiry

To cultivate a culture of inquiry, it is essential to address and overcome the fears that inhibit questioning. Here are several strategies to encourage open dialogue and empower individuals to ask questions without hesitation:

1. **Create a Safe Environment:** Organizations and communities should strive to create an environment where questioning is encouraged and valued. This can be achieved by fostering a culture of psychological safety, where individuals feel secure in expressing their thoughts without fear of negative consequences.

2. **Lead by Example:** Leaders and influential figures should model the behavior they wish to see by asking questions openly and embracing inquiry. When leaders demonstrate curiosity and vulnerability, it sets a tone that encourages others to follow suit.

3. **Normalize Questions:** Reinforce the idea that questions are a natural and vital part of learning and growth. By normalizing questioning, we can reduce the stigma associated with asking difficult or uncomfortable questions.

4. **Encourage Curiosity:** Foster a culture that values curiosity and exploration. Encourage individuals to embrace their innate curiosity and view questioning as an opportunity for growth rather than a challenge to authority.

5. **Provide Resources and Support:** Offer resources, workshops, or training sessions focused on effective questioning techniques. Empower individuals with the skills and confidence they need to articulate their concerns and seek answers.

6. **Acknowledge and Address Concerns:** Actively listen to individuals' fears and concerns about questioning. Acknowledging these feelings and addressing them openly can help reduce anxiety and build trust within the community.

7. **Celebrate Inquiries and Discoveries**: Recognize and celebrate instances where questions lead to valuable insights or positive changes. By highlighting the benefits of inquiry, we reinforce its importance and motivate others to engage in questioning.

The Power of Asking Questions

When we overcome the fear of asking questions, we empower ourselves and those around us to seek truth and understanding. The act of questioning is not merely about challenging authority or confronting uncomfortable truths; it is about fostering a culture of openness, learning, and accountability. By encouraging inquiry, we can create environments that promote innovation, collaboration, and growth.

In personal relationships, asking questions can strengthen bonds and enhance communication. It allows individuals to express their thoughts and feelings openly, leading to deeper connections and mutual understanding. By nurturing a culture of inquiry within our relationships, we can cultivate trust and respect, essential components of any healthy interaction.

In professional contexts, the willingness to ask questions can lead to improved processes, increased efficiency, and greater employee satisfaction. Organizations that embrace inquiry foster an environment of collaboration, where employees feel valued and empowered to contribute their ideas and perspectives.

Conclusion

Asking questions is a fundamental aspect of human interaction and discovery. Despite the barriers created by fear, it is essential to recognize the importance of inquiry in our lives. By overcoming our fears and fostering a culture of questioning, we can drive meaningful change, promote growth, and seek truth in our personal and professional journeys.

Ultimately, the courage to ask questions is a testament to our commitment to understanding ourselves and the world around us. By embracing inquiry and challenging the status quo, we can cultivate a society that values knowledge, accountability, and open dialogue. In doing so, we not only empower ourselves but also inspire others to join us in the pursuit of truth and understanding.

XXIII

The True Spirit of Competition: Elevating Ourselves among Peers

In the journey of personal and professional growth, competition is often viewed as a driving force that propels individuals to excel. However, the nature of competition can sometimes lead us astray, especially when driven by ego and a desire to dominate those who are less experienced or less accomplished. Competing with individuals who are at the same level not only fosters genuine growth but also cultivates a spirit of collaboration and mutual respect. This essay delves into the importance of competing with peers, the pitfalls of ego-driven competition, and how to cultivate a mindset that prioritizes healthy competition and self-improvement.

Understanding Competition

Competition is an inherent part of human nature, rooted in our instinct to survive and thrive. It can manifest in various forms—academic, professional, athletic, or artistic—and serves as a catalyst for innovation, excellence, and progress. At its best, competition pushes individuals to exceed their limits, challenge themselves, and strive for improvement. However, it can also create a toxic environment when fueled by ego and a desire to dominate those perceived as lesser.

The Value of Competing with Peers

1. **Mutual Growth:** Competing with others at the same level creates an environment where all participants can learn from each other.

Peers can share insights, strategies, and experiences that contribute to collective growth. This collaborative approach fosters an atmosphere of support rather than one of hostility or resentment.

2. **Motivation and Inspiration:** Engaging with peers who share similar goals can be a significant source of motivation. Observing their achievements can inspire individuals to push their boundaries and strive for their best. Healthy competition encourages individuals to elevate their performance rather than simply striving to outdo those who are less experienced.

3. **Skill Development:** Competing on equal footing allows individuals to refine their skills and techniques in a constructive manner. It provides an opportunity to test one's abilities against those of peers, fostering a sense of camaraderie and shared learning experiences. This environment encourages participants to be more innovative and creative in their approaches.

4. **Accountability:** When individuals compete with peers, they hold each other accountable for their performance. This accountability helps maintain focus and encourages participants to commit fully to their goals, resulting in a more profound dedication to personal and professional development.

The Dangers of Ego-Driven Competition

1. **Disconnection from Values:** When competition is driven by ego, individuals may prioritize winning over learning. This focus on superficial success can lead to unethical behavior, such as sabotaging others or bending rules, which ultimately undermines personal integrity and growth.

2. **Stunted Growth:** Competing against those perceived as less accomplished can lead to complacency. When individuals only seek to outshine those beneath them, they miss out on valuable

opportunities for growth and improvement that come from engaging with peers who challenge them.

3. **Toxic Environments:** Ego-driven competition can foster a toxic atmosphere characterized by jealousy, resentment, and hostility. This environment can lead to stress, burnout, and disengagement, detracting from the overall experience and diminishing the joy of achievement.

4. **Limited Perspective:** When individuals focus on winning against those below their level, they may become closed off to new ideas and perspectives. Engaging with peers encourages diverse viewpoints and constructive feedback, enriching one's understanding and promoting growth.

Cultivating a Healthy Competitive Mindset

To embrace the true spirit of competition, individuals must cultivate a mindset that values growth, collaboration, and respect for peers. Here are several strategies to foster healthy competition:

1. **Shift the Focus to Self-Improvement:** Instead of comparing oneself to others, prioritize personal growth and development. Set individual goals and strive to exceed them, using peer competition as a means of motivation rather than a benchmark for success.

2. **Embrace Collaboration:** Seek opportunities for collaboration and teamwork with peers. Working together can lead to innovative solutions and deeper insights, reinforcing the idea that success is often a collective effort.

3. **Celebrate Others' Successes:** Instead of feeling threatened by the accomplishments of peers, celebrate their successes. Recognizing and appreciating others' achievements fosters a

sense of community and encourages a positive competitive atmosphere.

4. **Practice Empathy:** Understand that every individual is on their unique journey. Practicing empathy allows individuals to appreciate the challenges and experiences of their peers, fostering a sense of camaraderie rather than rivalry.

5. **Create Supportive Networks:** Build or join networks that emphasize collaboration and support among peers. These communities can provide a platform for sharing experiences, knowledge, and resources, promoting a healthy competitive spirit.

6. **Reflect on Motivations:** Regularly reflect on personal motivations for competing. Are you striving for improvement and growth, or are you seeking validation through dominance? Understanding your motivations can help redirect your competitive spirit toward healthier pursuits.

Conclusion

Competition, when approached with the right mindset, can be a powerful catalyst for growth and self-improvement. Competing with individuals at the same level allows for mutual learning, inspiration, and collaboration, creating an environment where all participants can thrive. However, the dangers of ego-driven competition—rooted in a desire to dominate those perceived as lesser—can stifle growth, create toxicity, and disconnect individuals from their core values.

To cultivate a spirit of healthy competition, individuals must prioritize personal growth, embrace collaboration, and celebrate the successes of their peers. By shifting the focus from winning against others to striving for collective improvement, we can create a more enriching and fulfilling competitive experience. Ultimately, the true spirit of competition lies not in outshining others but in elevating ourselves alongside our peers, fostering a culture of support, respect, and shared growth. Through this approach, we can harness the power of competition to propel ourselves forward while nurturing the connections that make our journeys meaningful.

XXIV

The Power of Gratitude: Recognizing Those Who Helped Us in Difficult Times

Gratitude is a profound emotion that connects us to others and deepens our understanding of our experiences. In times of struggle, the assistance we receive from friends, family, mentors, and even strangers can make a significant difference in our lives. Recognizing and appreciating their contributions is not only a moral obligation but also a vital aspect of personal growth and well-being. This essay explores the importance of gratitude, the consequences of forgetting those who have helped us, and practical ways to cultivate a mindset of appreciation.

Understanding the Importance of Gratitude

Gratitude is more than just saying "thank you." It is recognition of the support, kindness, and love we receive from others, particularly during challenging times. Acknowledging the help we receive can enhance our emotional health and foster stronger relationships. Here are several reasons why gratitude is crucial:

1. **Emotional Resilience:** Practicing gratitude helps build emotional resilience. During difficult times, focusing on the positive aspects of our experiences and the support we have received can provide comfort and strength. Gratitude enables

us to shift our perspective from despair to hope, reminding us that we are not alone in our struggles.

2. **Strengthening Relationships:** Expressing gratitude fosters deeper connections with others. When we acknowledge the help we receive, it reinforces our relationships and creates a sense of mutual respect and appreciation. This reciprocity enhances our social bonds and encourages others to continue offering their support.

3. **Enhancing Well-Being:** Research has shown that individuals who practice gratitude experience greater overall well-being. They report higher levels of happiness, reduced stress, and improved mental health. Gratitude can shift our focus from what we lack to what we have, cultivating a more positive outlook on life.

4. **Encouraging Generosity:** Recognizing and appreciating the help we receive can inspire us to pay it forward. When we feel grateful for the support we have received, we are more likely to extend our help to others in need. This creates a cycle of kindness and compassion within our communities.

The Consequences of Forgetting Gratitude

Forgetting those who have helped us during difficult times can have significant repercussions. Neglecting to acknowledge the contributions of others not only harms our relationships but can also hinder our personal growth. Here are some consequences of failing to practice gratitude:

1. **Erosion of Relationships:** When we overlook the support we receive, it can lead to feelings of resentment and disappointment among those who helped us. Relationships thrive on

acknowledgment and appreciation; neglecting to express gratitude can strain these connections and diminish trust.

2. **Isolation and Loneliness:** Forgetting to appreciate others can create a sense of isolation. When we fail to recognize the contributions of those around us, we may unintentionally push them away, leading to loneliness during times when we need support the most.

3. **Diminished Self-Awareness:** A lack of gratitude can hinder self-awareness and personal growth. Recognizing the support we receive helps us understand the value of community and connection. When we forget the efforts of others, we risk becoming self-centered and disconnected from the reality of our shared experiences.

4. **Self-Destruction:** Neglecting gratitude can ultimately lead to self-destruction. By failing to appreciate the support we receive, we may develop a sense of entitlement and lose touch with the values that foster compassion and empathy. This self-centered mindset can lead to burnout, dissatisfaction, and a lack of fulfillment in our lives.

Cultivating a Mindset of Gratitude

To avoid the pitfalls of forgetting those who have helped us, it is essential to cultivate a mindset of gratitude. Here are several practical strategies to foster appreciation in our lives:

1. **Keep a Gratitude Journal:** Maintaining a gratitude journal is a powerful way to reflect on the support we receive. Regularly writing down the names of those who have helped us and the specific contributions they made can reinforce our appreciation and serve as a reminder of our connections.

2. **Express Gratitude Verbally:** Take the time to express gratitude to those who have helped you. A simple "thank you" can go a long way in acknowledging their support. Whether it's through a heartfelt conversation, a handwritten note, or a public acknowledgment, expressing gratitude reinforces your appreciation.

3. **Reflect on Difficult Times:** Periodically reflect on past challenges and the people who stood by you during those times. This reflection can help you recognize the importance of their support and reinforce your commitment to appreciating them moving forward.

4. **Practice Mindfulness:** Mindfulness practices can enhance our awareness of the present moment and the people around us. By being present, we can better appreciate the support we receive and recognize opportunities to express gratitude.

5. **Create a Gratitude Ritual:** Establishing a regular gratitude ritual, such as sharing what you are grateful for during family meals or gatherings, can reinforce the importance of appreciation within your community. This practice encourages open dialogue about support and fosters a culture of gratitude.

6. **Pay It Forward:** Actively seek opportunities to help others in the same way you have been helped. By paying it forward, you demonstrate the importance of gratitude and contribute to a cycle of kindness within your community.

Conclusion

Gratitude is a powerful force that can profoundly impact our lives and relationships. Recognizing those who have helped us during difficult times is not only a moral obligation but also a vital component of emotional resilience, relationship-building, and personal growth.

Forgetting to appreciate the support we receive can lead to strained relationships, isolation, and ultimately self-destruction.

By cultivating a mindset of gratitude, we can strengthen our connections with others, enhance our well-being, and foster a culture of kindness and compassion. Practicing gratitude enables us to acknowledge the contributions of those around us and inspires us to extend our support to others in need. In doing so, we not only honor those who have helped us but also enrich our own lives and the lives of those in our communities. Ultimately, gratitude serves as a reminder that we are all interconnected, and it is through our shared experiences that we can navigate the challenges of life together.

XXV

Choosing Reaction over Action: The Power of Intentional Response

In our complex and often chaotic world, we are constantly faced with moral dilemmas and challenging situations. The way we respond to these challenges defines not only our character but also the outcomes of the situations we encounter. The phrase "Don't be a wrong action, rather be a reaction against wrong" encapsulates the essence of intentionality in our responses to injustice and wrongdoing. This essay delves into the significance of thoughtful reactions, the consequences of impulsive actions, and the ways we can cultivate a more reflective and constructive approach to addressing wrongs in our lives.

Understanding Action vs. Reaction

At its core, the distinction between action and reaction lies in the intention behind each. Action typically implies a proactive decision made with consideration and awareness, while reaction often connotes a spontaneous response driven by emotions or immediate circumstances. When we encounter wrongdoing, it is crucial to differentiate between these two approaches:

1. **Action:** This involves taking steps based on our values, principles, and thoughtful consideration of the situation. Actions stem from a place of intention and clarity, focusing on constructive outcomes.

2. **Reaction:** Conversely, reactions are often knee-jerk responses influenced by emotions such as anger, fear, or frustration. These can lead to impulsive behavior that may exacerbate the situation or create additional harm.

By consciously choosing to be a reaction against wrong rather than engaging in wrong actions ourselves, we position ourselves as agents of change rather than perpetuators of negativity.

The Consequences of Wrong Actions

Engaging in wrong actions—whether through unethical behavior, harm to others, or unproductive responses—can have far-reaching consequences. Some of the most significant impacts include:

1. **Perpetuating a Cycle of Harm:** When we respond to wrongdoing with further wrongdoing, we contribute to a cycle of negativity. This can escalate conflicts and lead to an environment filled with hostility and resentment.

2. **Loss of Integrity:** Acting wrongly can compromise our values and integrity. When we allow our emotions to dictate our actions, we risk losing sight of who we are and what we stand for, which can have lasting effects on our self-esteem and reputation.

3. **Deterioration of Relationships:** Wrong actions can strain relationships with others. When we lash out or respond impulsively, we can alienate those around us, creating rifts that may take significant time and effort to mend.

4. **Regret and Guilt:** Engaging in actions we later regret can lead to feelings of guilt and shame. This emotional burden can weigh heavily on our mental well-being and create an internal conflict that can be challenging to navigate.

5. **Missed Opportunities for Growth:** When we allow ourselves to react impulsively, we miss opportunities to learn and grow from the experience. Thoughtful reactions can lead to deeper understanding and personal development, while rash actions often result in stagnation.

The Importance of Thoughtful Reactions

Choosing to react thoughtfully to wrongdoing has numerous benefits. By intentionally considering our responses, we can create positive outcomes and foster an environment of understanding and respect. Here are some key reasons why thoughtful reactions matter:

1. **Promoting Positive Change:** Thoughtful reactions can serve as catalysts for positive change. By addressing wrongdoing constructively, we can inspire others to reflect on their actions and make better choices, leading to a ripple effect of positive behavior.

2. **Fostering Understanding:** Responding thoughtfully allows us to seek understanding rather than simply reacting in anger. By approaching a situation with empathy, we create space for dialogue and exploration of different perspectives, fostering deeper connections with others.

3. **Building Resilience:** Thoughtful reactions require self-reflection and emotional regulation, skills that contribute to personal resilience. By practicing restraint and intentionality, we strengthen our ability to navigate challenging situations in the future.

4. **Enhancing Problem-Solving Skills:** When we take the time to respond thoughtfully, we engage in critical thinking and creative problem-solving. This approach allows us to explore

various solutions rather than defaulting to impulsive reactions that may not address the core issue.

5. **Maintaining Personal Integrity**: Choosing to react against wrong rather than engage in wrong actions helps us maintain our integrity. By upholding our values and principles, we reinforce our commitment to being a positive force in the world.

Strategies for Cultivating Thoughtful Reactions

Developing the ability to react thoughtfully requires practice and intention. Here are several strategies to help cultivate this skill:

1. **Pause and Reflect:** When faced with a situation that evokes strong emotions, take a moment to pause and reflect before responding. This can help you gain clarity and perspective, allowing you to respond more intentionally.

2. **Practice Emotional Regulation:** Develop techniques to manage your emotions effectively. This could include mindfulness practices, deep breathing exercises, or journaling to process your feelings before reacting.

3. **Seek Understanding:** Approach situations with curiosity rather than judgment. Ask questions and seek to understand the perspectives of others involved. This can lead to more constructive and empathetic responses.

4. **Consider the Consequences:** Before responding, consider the potential outcomes of your actions. Ask yourself how your reaction will impact the situation and the people involved, allowing this awareness to guide your response.

5. **Focus on Solutions:** Rather than dwelling on the problem, shift your focus to potential solutions. What can you do to address

the wrongdoing constructively? This proactive approach can lead to more positive outcomes.

6. **Surround Yourself with Support:** Engage with people who encourage thoughtful responses and constructive dialogue. A supportive community can help reinforce your commitment to reacting thoughtfully rather than impulsively.

7. **Reflect on Past Experiences:** Take time to reflect on past situations where you reacted impulsively. What were the outcomes? What could you have done differently? Learning from these experiences can help you develop a more thoughtful approach in the future.

Conclusion

The phrase "Don't be a wrong action, rather be a reaction against wrong" serves as a powerful reminder of the importance of intentionality in our responses to wrongdoing. Choosing to react thoughtfully not only fosters personal growth and resilience but also promotes positive change and understanding within our communities. By recognizing the consequences of impulsive actions and cultivating a mindset focused on constructive reactions, we can position ourselves as agents of positive change.

In a world where challenges and injustices abound, our ability to respond thoughtfully can make a significant difference. By embracing the power of intentional reactions, we contribute to a culture of empathy, respect, and growth. Ultimately, the choice between action and reaction lies within us, and by choosing wisely, we can shape our own paths while positively influencing the world around us.

XXVI

Embracing Mistakes: The Path to Self-Discovery and Growth

In our journey through life, we often encounter challenges and setbacks that test our resilience and character. One of the most significant obstacles we face is the internal struggle with our mistakes. An "enemy within" can manifest as self-doubt, fear, or a desire to hide our shortcomings. However, the path to personal growth and self-improvement lies in confronting these mistakes head-on, rather than covering them up. This essay explores the importance of introspection, the consequences of hiding our mistakes, and the strategies we can adopt to turn our failures into opportunities for growth.

Understanding the Enemy Within

The concept of an enemy within us refers to the negative thoughts and emotions that can sabotage our efforts to grow and improve. This internal adversary often leads us to:

1. **Deny Responsibility:** When we make mistakes, our first instinct might be to shift the blame onto external factors or others. This denial prevents us from taking ownership of our actions and learning from them.

2. **Fear Judgment:** We may fear how others will perceive us if we acknowledge our mistakes. This fear can lead to hiding our failures, perpetuating a cycle of shame and self-doubt.

3. **Avoid Introspection:** The enemy within often discourages introspection, as examining our mistakes can be uncomfortable. We may avoid reflecting on our actions to escape feelings of guilt or inadequacy.

4. **Strive for Perfection:** Many of us are conditioned to seek perfection and view mistakes as failures. This mindset can create immense pressure, leading us to conceal our shortcomings rather than embracing them as opportunities for growth.

The Consequences of Covering Mistakes

Hiding our mistakes can have serious repercussions that extend beyond the individual. Some of the most significant consequences include:

1. **Stunted Personal Growth:** When we cover our mistakes, we miss out on valuable learning opportunities. Each mistake contains lessons that can lead to self-improvement, innovation, and resilience. By avoiding introspection, we limit our potential for growth.

2. **Increased Anxiety and Stress:** Concealing mistakes creates a heavy emotional burden. The fear of discovery and the effort required to maintain the facade can lead to heightened anxiety and stress, affecting our mental and physical well-being.

3. **Erosion of Trust:** When we hide our mistakes from others, we risk eroding trust in our relationships. Authenticity and vulnerability foster deeper connections, while deceit and avoidance create barriers that hinder meaningful interactions.

4. **Reinforcement of Negative Patterns:** Covering mistakes can lead to a cycle of avoidance, where we repeatedly fail to address our shortcomings. This cycle can perpetuate negative behaviors and prevent us from making the necessary changes to improve.

5. **Loss of Authenticity:** When we conceal our mistakes, we present a curated version of ourselves to the world, which can lead to a disconnection from our true selves. Authenticity is essential for meaningful relationships and personal fulfillment.

The Importance of Introspection

Introspection is the practice of examining our thoughts, feelings, and actions in a reflective manner. This self-exploration is crucial for personal growth and development. Here are several reasons why introspection matters:

1. **Ownership and Accountability:** Introspection allows us to take ownership of our mistakes. Acknowledging our role in a situation empowers us to make conscious decisions to improve and learn from our experiences.

2. **Clarity and Understanding:** Reflecting on our mistakes provides clarity about our motivations and behaviors. Understanding the underlying causes of our actions helps us avoid repeating them in the future.

3. **Emotional Processing:** Introspection provides a safe space for processing emotions associated with our mistakes. By allowing ourselves to feel and understand our emotions, we can move towards healing and growth.

4. **Encouragement of Growth Mindset:** Embracing mistakes as opportunities for growth fosters a growth mindset. This perspective encourages resilience and adaptability, allowing us to approach challenges with confidence and determination.

5. **Improved Decision-Making:** By learning from past mistakes, we enhance our decision-making skills. Introspection equips us with the insights necessary to navigate future challenges more effectively.

Strategies for Introspection and Growth

Cultivating a habit of introspection and turning mistakes into learning experiences requires conscious effort. Here are several strategies to help you embrace this process:

1. **Create a Reflection Routine:** Set aside dedicated time for reflection, whether through journaling, meditation, or quiet contemplation. Regular reflection allows you to process your experiences and identify areas for improvement.

2. **Ask Constructive Questions:** When examining a mistake, ask yourself questions that promote understanding and growth. Consider what led to the mistake, how it made you feel, and what you can learn from the experience.

3. **Seek Feedback from Others:** Engaging with trusted friends, family, or mentors can provide valuable perspectives on your mistakes. Constructive feedback can help you gain insights and identify blind spots in your thinking.

4. **Practice Self-Compassion:** Be kind to yourself during the introspection process. Recognize that everyone makes mistakes and that imperfection is a natural part of being human. Self-compassion encourages growth rather than self-criticism.

5. **Set Goals for Improvement:** After reflecting on your mistakes, set specific, achievable goals for improvement. This proactive approach can help you stay focused on growth and motivate you to implement positive changes in your life.

6. **Embrace Vulnerability:** Share your experiences and mistakes with others. Embracing vulnerability fosters deeper connections and creates a supportive environment where others feel comfortable sharing their challenges as well.

7. **Celebrate Progress:** Acknowledge and celebrate the steps you take toward personal growth. Recognizing your progress reinforces the importance of introspection and encourages you to continue on this journey.

Conclusion

The internal struggle with mistakes can be one of the most challenging aspects of personal growth. An enemy within us may tempt us to cover up our shortcomings, leading to denial, anxiety, and missed opportunities for learning. However, the path to self-discovery and growth lies in embracing our mistakes through introspection and reflection.

By confronting our errors with honesty and courage, we empower ourselves to learn, evolve, and become better versions of ourselves. Introspection is not merely an exercise in self-criticism; it is a powerful tool for understanding, healing, and growth. Ultimately, by choosing to turn our mistakes into opportunities for improvement, we can transform our lives and inspire those around us to do the same. Embracing our imperfections allows us to cultivate authenticity, resilience, and a deeper connection to ourselves and others, paving the way for a more fulfilling and meaningful life.

XXVII

The Perils of Daydreaming: Chasing Pink Dreams

In a world filled with distractions and possibilities, it is all too easy to succumb to the allure of daydreaming. We often find ourselves drifting into a realm of idealized scenarios, envisioning lives filled with happiness, success, and fulfillment. However, these "pink dreams" can lead us astray, ultimately setting us up for disappointment and disillusionment. This essay explores the dangers of daydreaming, the importance of grounding our aspirations in reality, and strategies to transform our dreams into actionable goals.

Understanding Daydreaming and Pink Dreams

Daydreaming is a natural human tendency that allows us to escape reality and explore our fantasies. While it can provide temporary relief from stress and inspire creativity, excessive daydreaming often morphs into "pink dreams"—idealistic visions that are disconnected from the realities of our lives. These dreams are characterized by:

1. **Unrealistic Expectations:** Pink dreams often reflect a version of reality that is overly optimistic and unattainable. They create a false narrative that can lead to disappointment when the outcomes do not match our fantasies.

2. **Avoidance of Reality:** Daydreaming can serve as a coping mechanism, allowing us to avoid confronting difficult situations or emotions. By escaping into our fantasies, we may

neglect important responsibilities and challenges that require our attention.

3. **Stagnation:** When we become too immersed in our pink dreams, we may become complacent, believing that our aspirations will come to fruition without effort. This complacency can hinder our progress and prevent us from taking the necessary steps to achieve our goals.

4. **Disconnection from the Present:** Daydreaming can create a sense of disconnection from reality, leading us to overlook the opportunities and challenges that exist in our present lives. This disconnect can hinder personal growth and fulfillment.

The Consequences of Chasing Pink Dreams

While daydreaming may seem harmless, the consequences of pursuing unrealistic aspirations can be significant:

1. **Disappointment and Frustration:** When our idealized visions do not materialize, we may experience disappointment and frustration. This can lead to feelings of inadequacy and self-doubt, as we question our abilities and worth.

2. **Loss of Motivation:** Continuously chasing unattainable dreams can result in a loss of motivation. When we invest our energy in fantasies rather than actionable goals, we may become disheartened and disengaged from our pursuits.

3. **Missed Opportunities:** Being lost in daydreams can cause us to overlook opportunities that are present in our lives. By failing to engage with the present moment, we may miss out on valuable experiences and connections.

4. **Emotional Turmoil:** The disparity between our pink dreams and reality can lead to emotional turmoil. The constant struggle

between aspiration and reality can create anxiety and contribute to a cycle of negative emotions.

5. **Neglect of Responsibilities:** Daydreaming can distract us from our responsibilities, leading to unfulfilled commitments and a lack of progress in our personal and professional lives. This neglect can have long-term consequences on our relationships and well-being.

The Importance of Grounding Aspirations in Reality

To achieve true fulfillment, it is essential to ground our aspirations in reality. Here are several reasons why this approach is crucial:

1. **Realistic Goal Setting:** By setting achievable goals based on our current circumstances, we can create a clear path toward success. Realistic goals provide us with a sense of direction and purpose, motivating us to take actionable steps.

2. **Embracing Challenges:** Confronting reality allows us to embrace challenges and setbacks as part of the growth process. Rather than avoiding difficulties, we learn to navigate obstacles and develop resilience.

3. **Fostering Personal Growth:** Grounding our aspirations in reality encourages personal growth. By acknowledging our limitations and areas for improvement, we can work on developing the skills and attributes necessary to achieve our goals.

4. **Cultivating Gratitude:** Engaging with reality fosters gratitude for the present moment. When we focus on what we have and the progress we've made, we cultivate a positive mindset that enhances our overall well-being.

5. **Building Authentic Connections:** Grounding our aspirations in reality helps us build authentic connections with others.

By sharing our genuine experiences and challenges, we create opportunities for meaningful relationships and support.

Strategies for Transforming Dreams into Actionable Goals

To turn daydreams into actionable goals, we must adopt a proactive approach. Here are several strategies to help transform our aspirations into reality:

1. **Practice Self-Reflection:** Take time to reflect on your dreams and aspirations. Identify which ones are grounded in reality and which are idealized fantasies. This reflection will help clarify your goals and aspirations.

2. **Set SMART Goals:** Utilize the SMART criteria—Specific, Measurable, Achievable, Relevant, and Time-bound—to set clear and actionable goals. This structured approach provides a roadmap for achieving your aspirations.

3. **Break down Goals:** Divide larger goals into smaller, manageable steps. Breaking goals down into achievable tasks makes them less overwhelming and provides a sense of accomplishment as you progress.

4. **Create an Action Plan:** Develop a concrete action plan that outlines the steps you need to take to achieve your goals. This plan should include timelines, resources, and potential obstacles, allowing you to stay organized and focused.

5. **Embrace Flexibility:** While it's important to stay committed to your goals, be open to adjusting your plans as circumstances change. Embracing flexibility allows you to adapt to new challenges and seize unexpected opportunities.

6. **Seek Support:** Surround yourself with individuals who encourage and support your aspirations. Sharing your goals

with others can create accountability and provide valuable insights and encouragement along the way.

7. **Celebrate Progress:** Acknowledge and celebrate your achievements, no matter how small. Recognizing your progress fosters motivation and reinforces your commitment to pursuing your goals.

Conclusion

Daydreaming can be a double-edged sword. While it offers an escape and sparks creativity, it can also lead to unrealistic expectations and a disconnection from reality. The pursuit of "pink dreams" can result in disappointment, frustration, and stagnation. To achieve true fulfillment, it is crucial to ground our aspirations in reality, embracing challenges and setbacks as opportunities for growth.

By transforming our dreams into actionable goals and adopting a proactive approach to our aspirations, we can create a path toward personal growth and success. Engaging with reality allows us to cultivate gratitude, build authentic connections, and navigate life's challenges with resilience. Ultimately, the key to fulfillment lies in our ability to balance our dreams with a grounded approach to reality, enabling us to create the life we truly desire.

XXVIII

The Importance of Remembering: Confronting Personal and Societal Challenges

In the fast-paced, ever-changing world we live in, it is easy to become disconnected from the past. Whether it's a personal hardship or a societal injustice, our tendency is to move on, often forgetting the deep impact these experiences have on us and the people around us. However, forgetting can be dangerous. It is crucial to remember what has affected us and society so that we can actively work to resolve these issues. The mind's natural tendency to push painful memories aside may lead to complacency, but true progress requires us to confront these challenges head-on.

This essay explores the importance of remembering, the dangers of forgetting, and the steps we can take to actively resolve the issues that continue to affect us and the society we live in.

The Tendency to Forget

The human mind is wired to protect itself from emotional and psychological distress. One way it does this is by encouraging us to forget or distance ourselves from difficult memories. Whether it's a personal trauma or a broader societal issue like discrimination, economic disparity, or environmental degradation, the mind often prefers to suppress painful experiences rather than confront them. This tendency to forget serves as a defense mechanism that allows us to continue functioning in our daily lives without being overwhelmed by past events.

However, this tendency to forget comes at a price. By ignoring or pushing aside what has affected us, we risk allowing these issues to remain unresolved. When personal or societal problems are left unaddressed, they often resurface in different forms, creating a cycle of pain, confusion, and dysfunction. Suppression may provide temporary relief, but it does not lead to healing or resolution.

Why It Is Important to Remember

1. **Learning from the Past:** Remembering allows us to learn from our mistakes and past experiences. Both on a personal level and as a society, mistakes can serve as valuable lessons. Whether it's understanding how a decision led to negative consequences or how systemic issues have hurt certain groups, remembering these events provides the foundation for growth and change.

2. **Fostering Accountability:** On a societal level, remembering injustices and crises ensures that those responsible are held accountable. Forgetting societal issues like corruption, human rights violations, or environmental degradation allows the perpetrators to continue their harmful behaviors unchecked. Similarly, on a personal level, forgetting the people or circumstances that have hurt us allows toxic relationships or harmful habits to persist.

3. **Building Resilience:** Remembering personal and societal challenges also builds resilience. Acknowledging what we have gone through helps us to prepare for similar challenges in the future. As the saying goes, "Those who do not learn from history are doomed to repeat it." The same applies on a personal level. When we remember how we overcame obstacles, it strengthens our ability to face future challenges with greater confidence and wisdom.

4. **Healing:** Suppressing painful experiences doesn't heal wounds; it merely covers them up. Real healing requires confronting and processing these events. By remembering what has affected us, we give ourselves the opportunity to truly resolve the emotional or psychological scars that may have been left behind. The same is true for societal healing. A nation that fails to remember and address its dark past, whether it involves slavery, colonization, or systemic inequality, cannot fully heal or progress.

The Dangers of Forgetting

The tendency to forget painful or difficult experiences is not just a personal issue; it is a societal one as well. Some of the dangers of forgetting include:

1. **Repeating Mistakes:** If we do not remember our past errors or societal failings, we risk repeating them. This is especially true in the context of history. Many of the conflicts, crises, and injustices we face today have roots in forgotten or ignored issues. Whether it's racial inequality, climate change, or economic disparity, failing to remember and address these systemic problems only leads to their perpetuation.

2. **Complacency:** Forgetting often leads to complacency. When we move on from difficult experiences without resolving them, we may become passive in the face of future challenges. For example, societal issues like corruption, inequality, or political instability may worsen if people forget their impact and stop demanding change. In personal relationships, forgetting how we've been hurt can allow toxic dynamics to continue unchecked.

3. **Undermining Progress**: Forgetting not only risks perpetuating harm but also undermines the progress that has been made. Societal advancements in civil rights, environmental protection

and healthcare can be easily rolled back if people forget the struggles that led to these achievements. On a personal level, forgetting past challenges can erode the growth and self-awareness we've cultivated through overcoming them.

How to Remember and Resolve Issues

Remembering and addressing personal and societal challenges is not easy, but it is necessary for growth, healing, and progress. Here are some strategies for actively confronting and resolving the issues that affect us:

1. **Create Space for Reflection:** Regularly take time to reflect on your personal experiences and the state of the world around you. Journaling, meditation, and conversations with others can help you process and remember significant events.

2. **Seek Out Knowledge:** Educate yourself about societal issues and the historical context behind them. Remembering isn't just about personal experiences; it's about being informed and aware of the larger forces at play. Books, documentaries, and academic resources can provide valuable insight into past societal issues and their current relevance.

3. **Engage in Dialogue:** Conversations with others, whether friends, family, or community members, can help keep memories of personal and societal challenges alive. Engaging in discussions about past experiences ensures that they are not forgotten and that they are addressed with collective wisdom.

4. **Take Action:** The most important part of remembering is resolving the issues that have affected you. On a personal level, this may mean seeking therapy, setting boundaries, or making lifestyle changes. On a societal level, it may mean getting

involved in activism, voting for leaders who address the issues, or working within your community to create change.

Conclusion

The tendency to forget what has affected us and society is a natural but dangerous part of the human experience. While the mind may encourage us to move on, true growth, healing, and progress require us to remember and resolve the issues that shape our lives. By engaging in introspection, education, dialogue, and action, we can confront both personal and societal challenges head-on. In doing so, we create the possibility for lasting change and a brighter, more resilient future.

XXIX

Breaking Free from Complacency: The Dangers of Adjusting to Inconvenience

In our daily lives, we often find ourselves adjusting to various inconveniences, whether they are personal, professional, or societal. This tendency to accommodate discomfort, inefficiencies, or even unfairness is often driven by the desire to maintain peace, avoid conflict, or simply because we have become accustomed to a particular situation. While this attitude may seem harmless on the surface, it can have long-term negative consequences for our well-being, personal growth, and the society we live in. This essay explores the dangers of adjusting to inconvenience, why we need to break free from this mindset, and how we can foster an attitude of active change and self-advocacy.

Understanding the Attitude of Adjustment

Adjustment is often viewed as a positive trait. Flexibility, compromise, and the ability to adapt to changing circumstances are valuable skills in both personal and professional life. However, there is a fine line between healthy adaptability and the passive acceptance of inconvenience. The latter often manifests as complacency, where individuals tolerate suboptimal conditions rather than seeking change. Some common reasons why people adjust to inconvenience include:

1. **Fear of Conflict:** Many people avoid addressing inconvenient situations because they fear conflict. Confronting problems

head-on may lead to uncomfortable conversations, disagreements, or even broken relationships. In an effort to avoid such outcomes, individuals often choose to quietly adjust, even when they are unhappy or uncomfortable.

2. **Desire for Stability:** People often prefer the familiarity of inconvenience over the uncertainty of change. Change can be daunting, and the unknown may seem riskier than continuing to tolerate an inconvenient situation. This desire for stability can lead to a mindset where people accept discomfort because they believe it's the safer option.

3. **Normalization of Inconvenience:** Over time, people can become desensitized to inconvenience. When minor irritations or inefficiencies are not addressed, they gradually become part of everyday life. What was once a source of frustration may become so normalized that it no longer seems like a problem worth solving.

4. **Low Self-Worth:** Some individuals adjust to inconvenience because they believe they do not deserve better. This is often rooted in low self-esteem or feelings of inadequacy, where people feel they have no right to demand more comfort, fairness, or happiness.

5. **Social and Cultural Expectations:** In many societies, people are conditioned to accept certain inconveniences as part of life. For example, workers may accept unfair treatment in the workplace because they believe it's just the nature of the job, or individuals may tolerate inequality in relationships because they have been taught that sacrifice is a virtue.

The Dangers of Adjusting to Inconvenience

While adjusting to inconvenience may provide temporary relief or help maintain peace, it can have serious long-term consequences. The dangers of this attitude extend beyond personal discomfort and can negatively impact mental health, relationships, career growth, and even societal progress.

1. Erosion of Self-Worth

Consistently adjusting to inconvenience can erode one's sense of self-worth and self-respect. When individuals regularly tolerate discomfort, unfair treatment, or substandard conditions, they begin to internalize the belief that they do not deserve better. This erosion of self-worth can lead to feelings of helplessness, resignation, and a diminished sense of personal power. Over time, individuals may lose the confidence to advocate for themselves or pursue opportunities for improvement, both in their personal and professional lives.

2. Stifled Personal Growth

Personal growth requires stepping outside of one's comfort zone and confronting challenges head-on. When individuals adjust to inconvenience, they often shy away from these necessary challenges, choosing instead to remain in situations that are familiar but uncomfortable. This avoidance of discomfort can stifle growth, as individuals miss out on opportunities to learn, develop new skills, and gain valuable experiences. Growth comes from pushing boundaries and seeking solutions, not from passively accepting unfavorable conditions.

3. Strain on Relationships

In personal relationships, the habit of adjusting to inconvenience can create strain and resentment. Whether it's tolerating a partner's unfair behavior, staying silent about unmet needs, or constantly compromising to maintain harmony, adjusting to inconvenience in relationships often leads to dissatisfaction. Over time, this can cause relationships to become imbalanced, with one party continuously sacrificing their own needs for the sake of the other. This dynamic can ultimately lead to frustration, resentment, and even the breakdown of the relationship.

4. Workplace Burnout and Career Stagnation

In professional settings, adjusting to inconvenience can lead to burnout and career stagnation. Workers who accept unreasonable workloads, toxic work environments, or a lack of recognition may experience chronic stress, exhaustion, and diminished job satisfaction. Additionally, the habit of adjusting to inconvenience in the workplace can prevent individuals from seeking promotions, raises, or career changes that could improve their professional lives. In the long term, this can result in a stagnant career trajectory and a lack of fulfillment in one's work.

5. Hindrance to Societal Progress

On a broader scale, the widespread acceptance of inconvenience can hinder societal progress. When individuals tolerate systemic inefficiencies, inequalities, or injustices, they contribute to the perpetuation of these problems. For example, if workers consistently adjust to unfair labor practices, employers have little incentive to improve working conditions. Similarly, when citizens adjust to corrupt governance or social inequalities, societal issues remain unresolved, preventing meaningful progress and reform.

Breaking Free from the Attitude of Adjustment

To foster a healthier and more proactive approach to inconvenience, individuals must cultivate the mindset and skills necessary to address and resolve uncomfortable situations. Here are some strategies for breaking free from the attitude of adjustment:

1. Recognize and Acknowledge Inconvenience

The first step toward change is recognizing and acknowledging the inconvenience. This requires self-awareness and a willingness to confront discomfort rather than brushing it aside. Whether it's a minor annoyance or a significant issue, acknowledging that a problem exists is essential for addressing it.

2. Set Boundaries

In personal and professional relationships, setting clear boundaries is crucial for preventing the habit of adjusting to inconvenience. Establishing boundaries communicates that your comfort, well-being, and needs matter. Boundaries also create the framework for healthy relationships, where mutual respect and fairness are prioritized.

3. Develop Assertiveness

Assertiveness is the ability to express your needs, desires, and concerns clearly and respectfully. Developing assertiveness allows individuals to advocate for themselves without resorting to aggression or passivity. It's an essential skill for addressing inconvenience and ensuring that your voice is heard.

4. Embrace Discomfort as a Catalyst for Change

Rather than avoiding discomfort, embrace it as a catalyst for change. Recognize that addressing inconvenient situations may involve difficult conversations or temporary discomfort, but the long-term benefits of resolving the issue far outweigh the short-term unease.

5. Challenge Social and Cultural Norms

On a societal level, challenging ingrained social and cultural norms is essential for addressing systemic inconvenience and inequality. This requires questioning long-held beliefs and practices that perpetuate unfairness and speaking out against injustices that have become normalized.

Conclusion

The tendency to adjust to inconvenience may seem like a harmless coping mechanism, but it can have profound negative effects on personal growth, relationships, professional development, and societal progress. Breaking free from this attitude requires self-awareness, assertiveness, and a willingness to embrace discomfort for the sake of meaningful change. By refusing to passively accept inconvenience, we can foster a culture of self-advocacy, fairness, and continuous growth, both for ourselves and for the world around us.

XXX

The Power of Consistency: Overcoming the Vulnerability of an Inconsistent Mind for Higher Achievements

The human mind, by its very nature, is prone to inconsistency. Our thoughts, emotions, and motivations can fluctuate daily, driven by external factors like stress, distractions, and changing environments. This mental variability often leads to inconsistency in our actions, which can hinder personal growth, career success, and overall fulfillment in life. Despite this natural vulnerability, the key to unlocking higher achievements lies in practicing and mastering consistency. In this essay, we will explore the concept of mental inconsistency, why it occurs, how it affects personal and professional goals, and most importantly, how practicing consistency can lead to sustained success and higher achievements.

The Inconsistent Nature of the Human Mind

The human mind is an intricate and complex system that constantly processes information from both internal and external stimuli. Emotions, thoughts, and desires ebb and flow in response to these stimuli, which makes it difficult to maintain a steady course of action. There are several reasons why our minds tend to be inconsistent:

1. Emotional Fluctuations

Emotions are one of the primary drivers of inconsistency in human behavior. On some days, we feel energized, motivated, and ready to tackle challenges, while on others, we might feel overwhelmed, anxious, or simply unmotivated. These emotional ups and downs affect our ability to maintain focus and follow through on tasks, leading to erratic performance.

2. Cognitive Overload

In today's fast-paced world, we are constantly bombarded with information. The mind can easily become overwhelmed by the sheer volume of tasks, decisions, and thoughts that need attention. Cognitive overload leads to mental fatigue, causing inconsistency in decision-making and the ability to concentrate on long-term goals.

3. Distractions

Distractions, both external and internal, play a significant role in disrupting consistency. Whether it's the lure of social media, unexpected interruptions, or fleeting thoughts that divert our attention, distractions cause us to veer off course and lose momentum in our efforts.

4. Lack of Discipline

Discipline is the backbone of consistency. However, maintaining discipline is challenging because the human mind naturally seeks comfort and avoids discomfort. Consistency often requires doing tasks that are not immediately gratifying, and without discipline, it's easy to abandon efforts when they become tedious or difficult.

5. Fear of Failure

The fear of failure can also lead to inconsistency. When we encounter setbacks or challenges, the instinctive reaction is often to retreat or abandon the task altogether. This fear-driven response prevents us from maintaining steady progress and reaching our full potential.

6. Changing Desires and Interests

As humans, our interests and desires evolve over time. What excites us one day may lose its appeal the next. This natural tendency to shift our focus can result in abandoning goals prematurely or jumping from one project to another without achieving mastery in any one area.

The Impact of Inconsistency on Achievements

Inconsistency in behavior and effort can have far-reaching consequences on our ability to achieve success. Whether in personal development, academic pursuits, professional goals, or relationships, inconsistency undermines progress and prevents individuals from reaching their full potential. Some of the key impacts include:

1. Lack of Progress

Inconsistency is the enemy of progress. When we fail to maintain steady effort, we halt our momentum and undo the gains we've made. This can lead to a cycle of starting and stopping, where little to no progress is achieved in the long run.

2. Erosion of Trust and Credibility

Inconsistency in professional settings, such as missing deadlines or failing to deliver on promises, can erode trust and damage one's reputation. Colleagues, clients, and employers are less likely to rely on someone who is unpredictable in their performance. This can have a significant negative impact on career advancement.

3. Missed Opportunities

Inconsistent behavior often leads to missed opportunities. For example, an individual who fails to consistently work on their skills or network with others may miss out on opportunities for promotions, partnerships, or personal growth. Success often requires being in the right place at the right time, and inconsistency makes it difficult to be prepared when opportunity knocks.

4. Diminished Self-Confidence

Inconsistency can also chip away at self-confidence. When individuals fail to achieve their goals due to inconsistent effort, they may begin to doubt their abilities and develop a negative self-image. This lack of self-belief further perpetuates the cycle of inconsistency, as individuals become less likely to commit to new challenges.

5. Unfulfilled Potential

The most significant impact of inconsistency is unfulfilled potential. Every individual has the capacity to achieve greatness in their chosen field, but without consistent effort, that potential remains unrealized. This leads to feelings of regret and dissatisfaction, as individuals look back on missed chances for growth and success.

The Power of Consistency in Achieving Success

While the human mind may be naturally inclined towards inconsistency, consistency is the foundation of all meaningful achievements. Consistency, when practiced deliberately, creates a stable platform for growth, improvement, and eventual success. Here's how consistency plays a crucial role in higher achievements:

1. Building Momentum

Consistency builds momentum over time. When we take small, consistent steps toward a goal, each step builds upon the previous one, creating a compounding effect. This momentum makes it easier to stay on track, as progress becomes visible and reinforces the motivation to continue.

2. Mastery through Repetition

Mastery in any field requires repetition and sustained effort. Whether learning a new skill, developing expertise in a profession, or cultivating healthy habits, consistency allows for the repetition necessary to achieve mastery. Without consistency, learning remains superficial, and true proficiency is never attained.

3. Establishing Discipline

Consistency fosters discipline, which is essential for overcoming distractions and emotional fluctuations. By practicing consistent behavior, individuals develop the ability to stay focused even when motivation wanes. Discipline is like a muscle that grows stronger with use, enabling individuals to push through challenges and resist the temptation to quit.

4. Building Trust and Reliability

In professional and personal relationships, consistency is the foundation of trust. When individuals consistently show up, meet expectations, and deliver results, they build a reputation for reliability. This trust opens doors to new opportunities, collaborations, and advancements, as people are more likely to invest in those they can count on.

5. Incremental Improvement

One of the greatest benefits of consistency is the power of incremental improvement. Even small, seemingly insignificant efforts can lead to substantial results over time when done consistently. For example, writing just one page a day can result in a completed book within a year. Similarly, consistent practice in any area, whether it's exercise, skill development, or professional work, leads to gradual improvement that compounds over time.

6. Resilience in the Face of Setbacks

Consistency also builds resilience. When individuals are consistent in their efforts, they become better equipped to handle setbacks and failures. Rather than giving up in the face of adversity, they are more likely to persist because they have developed the habit of steady effort. This resilience is a key factor in achieving long-term success, as it enables individuals to stay the course even when challenges arise.

Practicing Consistency for Higher Achievements

Given the power of consistency, how can individuals overcome the natural vulnerability of the human mind and practice consistency in their daily lives? Here are some strategies to cultivate consistency and unlock higher achievements:

1. Set Clear, Specific Goals

To practice consistency, it's essential to have clear, specific goals. Vague or overly broad goals make it difficult to maintain focus and measure progress. By setting well-defined goals with actionable steps, individuals can create a roadmap for consistent effort.

2. Create a Routine

Routines are powerful tools for fostering consistency. By establishing a daily or weekly routine, individuals create a structure that reinforces consistent behavior. Routines minimize the need for decision-making and reduce the likelihood of distractions, making it easier to stay on track.

3. Start Small

Consistency doesn't require grand, sweeping changes. In fact, attempting to overhaul one's life all at once can lead to burnout and failure. Instead, start with small, manageable steps and gradually build upon them. Consistency in small actions leads to significant results over time.

4. Track Progress

Tracking progress is a powerful motivator for maintaining consistency. By documenting achievements, individuals can see the tangible results of their efforts, which reinforces the desire to continue. Whether it's through journaling, habit-tracking apps, or regular self-assessment, tracking progress helps keep individuals accountable to their goals.

5. Embrace Accountability

Accountability, whether to oneself or others, is a key factor in maintaining consistency. Sharing goals with a friend, mentor, or accountability partner creates external motivation to stay consistent. Similarly, setting personal milestones and regularly assessing progress helps maintain internal accountability.

6. Develop a Growth Mindset

A growth mindset, the belief that abilities and intelligence can be developed through effort, is essential for practicing consistency.

Individuals with a growth mindset view challenges and setbacks as opportunities for learning rather than reasons to quit. This mindset fosters resilience and encourages consistent effort, even in the face of obstacles.

7. Focus on the Process, Not Just the Outcome

While goals are important, focusing solely on the outcome can lead to frustration and inconsistency. Instead, focus on the process of consistent effort. By finding satisfaction in the daily work and incremental progress, individuals can stay motivated even when the ultimate goal seems far away.

Conclusion

The human mind, with its inherent vulnerability to inconsistency, can often derail efforts toward success and fulfillment. However, by practicing consistency, individuals can overcome this vulnerability and achieve higher levels of success. Consistency builds momentum, fosters discipline, and leads to mastery, resilience, and incremental improvement. By setting clear goals, creating routines, and embracing a growth mindset, individuals can cultivate consistency and unlock their full potential. In a world full of distractions and uncertainties, consistency is the key to long-term achievement and personal growth.

XXXI

Overcoming the Darkness Within: How Scientific Temperament Defeats the Mind's Greatest Enemy

The human mind is a complex and dynamic entity, capable of incredible feats of creativity, intelligence, and empathy. Yet, it is equally susceptible to darkness — a metaphorical state characterized by ignorance, fear, irrationality, and emotional turmoil. This darkness is one of the greatest enemies humans face, as it clouds judgment, fuels destructive behaviors, and creates a mental environment where negative emotions and beliefs can thrive. However, there is a powerful antidote to this darkness: the cultivation of a scientific temperament.

Scientific temperament refers to an attitude of inquiry, critical thinking, skepticism, and a reliance on evidence and reason. It is the opposite of ignorance and blind faith, as it seeks to understand the world through logic, experimentation, and empirical observation. In this essay, we will explore how the darkness of the human mind manifests, why it is so dangerous, and how developing a scientific temperament can help overcome these challenges, leading to clarity, wisdom, and personal growth.

The Nature of Mental Darkness

Mental darkness can take many forms, ranging from ignorance to emotional instability, irrational fears, and even harmful ideologies. It often manifests as a lack of understanding, where individuals are unable to see the bigger picture, question their assumptions, or think critically about the information they consume. Some common elements of mental darkness include:

1. Ignorance

Ignorance is one of the most pervasive forms of mental darkness. It occurs when individuals lack knowledge about the world or are misinformed. Ignorance leads to poor decision-making and a skewed understanding of reality. Moreover, ignorance can foster a sense of helplessness, as people feel unable to navigate complex problems or make informed choices.

2. Superstition and Irrational Beliefs

Superstition and irrational beliefs thrive in the absence of scientific reasoning. When individuals accept unverified claims, myths, or pseudoscience as truth, they are more likely to act on flawed assumptions. This can result in harmful behaviors, such as avoiding necessary medical treatments or adhering to discriminatory practices rooted in falsehoods.

3. Fear and Anxiety

Fear, especially when irrational or exaggerated, is another aspect of mental darkness. It can paralyze individuals, preventing them from taking necessary actions or exploring new opportunities. Fear of the unknown, failure, or rejection can severely limit personal and professional growth, trapping people in a state of mental and emotional inertia.

4. Dogma and Closed-Mindedness

Dogma — the unwillingness to question established beliefs or ideas — represent another form of mental darkness. Individuals, who adhere to rigid belief systems, whether religious, political, or cultural, often reject new information or ideas that challenge their worldview. This intellectual inflexibility stifles growth and prevents individuals from evolving with new knowledge or understanding.

5. Emotional Turmoil

Unchecked emotions, such as anger, jealousy, or resentment, can cloud judgment and lead to self-destructive behaviors. Emotional darkness manifests when individuals are unable to manage their emotional responses, leading to impulsive decisions and strained relationships. This mental state prevents rational thinking and inhibits self-awareness.

These manifestations of mental darkness are detrimental not only to personal well-being but also to the larger society, as they contribute to social divisions, conflict, and stagnation. To overcome this darkness, individuals must cultivate a mindset that values reason, evidence, and open-mindedness — the pillars of a scientific temperament.

The Power of Scientific Temperament

Scientific temperament is a way of thinking and approaching the world that prioritizes rationality, evidence-based reasoning, and a curiosity-driven quest for knowledge. It is not limited to scientists or academics but is a mindset that anyone can adopt to enhance their understanding of themselves and the world around them. By embracing scientific temperament, individuals can combat the mental darkness that impairs their ability to think clearly, make sound decisions, and grow as human beings.

1. Critical Thinking and Skepticism

At the core of scientific temperament is critical thinking — the ability to analyze information objectively and question assumptions. Critical thinking involves skepticism, which means not accepting things at face value and seeking evidence before forming beliefs. This approach is essential for overcoming ignorance, as it encourages individuals to evaluate the reliability of information and differentiate between credible sources and misinformation.

When people develop critical thinking skills, they are less likely to fall prey to irrational fears or superstitions. They are equipped to question pseudoscientific claims, resist conspiracy theories, and avoid making decisions based on emotional bias. In this way, critical thinking acts as a beacon of light in the darkness, guiding individuals toward truth and clarity.

2. Emotional Regulation and Objectivity

One of the major challenges of the human mind is its susceptibility to emotional influences. Emotions, while important for human experience, can cloud judgment when not managed properly. A scientific temperament encourages individuals to separate emotions from facts. While emotions are valid and need to be acknowledged, they should not dominate decision-making.

Scientific thinking promotes objectivity — the ability to view situations and problems without emotional distortion. When individuals approach problems with objectivity, they are more likely to find rational solutions that are in their best interest. They are also better equipped to manage stress, anxiety, and fear, as they understand that these emotions, while real, can be mitigated through rational action and evidence-based strategies.

3. Curiosity and Lifelong Learning

Another critical component of scientific temperament is curiosity — the desire to explore, question, and learn. Curiosity drives individuals to seek new knowledge, challenge existing beliefs, and expand their understanding of the world. This attitude is crucial for combating the stagnation that comes from closed-mindedness and dogma.

People with a curious mindset are constantly learning and adapting. They understand that knowledge is not static and that new discoveries can reshape their understanding of reality. This willingness to learn and grow helps individuals overcome the mental rigidity that often accompanies dogmatic beliefs. Moreover, curiosity fosters creativity, as individuals are more open to exploring new ideas, perspectives, and solutions.

4. Evidence-Based Decision-Making

One of the hallmarks of scientific temperament is the reliance on evidence to make decisions. Rather than relying on intuition, tradition, or hearsay, individuals who embrace scientific thinking seek empirical data and facts before drawing conclusions. This approach is particularly important in areas such as health, education, and public policy, where evidence-based decisions lead to better outcomes.

For example, in the realm of personal health, individuals who practice scientific thinking are more likely to trust medical advice based on clinical research rather than falling for unproven alternative treatments. In their careers, evidence-based decision-making enables individuals to evaluate risks and opportunities more effectively, leading to more informed and successful outcomes.

5. Openness to Change

Scientific temperament also fosters openness to change. The scientific method itself is based on the idea that knowledge evolves over time as new evidence emerges. People who adopt this mindset are willing to revise their beliefs and adapt to new circumstances when presented with compelling evidence. This flexibility is crucial for personal growth, as it allows individuals to break free from outdated ideas and move forward with a more accurate understanding of the world.

Openness to change also helps individuals overcome fear, particularly fear of the unknown. When people understand that change is a natural and necessary part of life, they become less resistant to it and more willing to embrace new opportunities, even if they come with uncertainty.

6. Rational Problem-Solving

In times of crisis or challenge, individuals with a scientific temperament are better equipped to navigate problems rationally. They approach issues systematically, breaking them down into manageable parts and analyzing potential solutions based on available evidence. This rational approach to problem-solving not only leads to more effective solutions but also reduces the stress and anxiety that often accompany difficult situations.

By practicing rational problem-solving, individuals can overcome the mental darkness of confusion and helplessness that often arises in challenging circumstances. Instead of feeling overwhelmed, they take a proactive, logical approach to finding solutions.

Practical Ways to Cultivate Scientific Temperament

Given the profound benefits of a scientific temperament, how can individuals develop this mindset in their daily lives? Here are some practical strategies:

1. Question Assumptions

Start by questioning the assumptions you hold, especially those that are deeply ingrained or taken for granted. Ask yourself whether there is evidence to support these beliefs and whether they still serve you.

2. Seek Out Diverse Perspectives

Expose yourself to different viewpoints and ideas. This helps prevent intellectual stagnation and encourages open-mindedness. Engage in discussions with people who hold different opinions, and be willing to adjust your perspective when presented with compelling evidence.

3. Practice Critical Thinking

When confronted with new information, practice analyzing it critically. Ask questions like: Is this claim supported by evidence? What are the potential biases of the source? Are there alternative explanations?

4. Prioritize Evidence over Emotion

In decision-making, strive to prioritize facts and data over emotional reactions. While emotions are important, they should not be the sole basis for decisions that have long-term consequences.

5. Adopt a Growth Mindset

Embrace the idea that knowledge and skills can be developed over time. Rather than viewing challenges as threats, see them as opportunities to learn and grow. Be open to changing your beliefs when presented with new evidence.

6. Stay Curious

Make a habit of lifelong learning. Whether through reading, taking courses, or engaging in intellectual discussions, continually seek to expand your knowledge and understanding of the world.

Conclusion

The darkness of the human mind — characterized by ignorance, fear, irrationality, and emotional turmoil — is one of humanity's greatest enemies. However, this darkness can be overcome by cultivating a scientific temperament. Through critical thinking, emotional regulation, curiosity, evidence-based decision-making, and openness to change, individuals can illuminate their minds, gain clarity, and achieve personal and intellectual growth. The journey toward scientific thinking is not just a path to knowledge, but a path to a more enlightened, empowered, and fulfilling life.

XXXII

Understanding Your Reach: The Importance of Self-Awareness in Achieving Success

In a world filled with constant comparison and competition, it's easy to fall into the trap of doing something simply because someone else has done it. Whether it's pursuing a particular career, adopting a specific lifestyle, or making significant life choices, the influence of others often shapes our decisions. However, what works for one person may not necessarily work for another. Every individual has unique abilities, capacities, and limitations that define what they can and cannot do effectively. Thus, blindly following someone else's path can lead to frustration, disappointment, and even failure.

The key to success is knowing yourself—your strengths, weaknesses, limitations, and potential. Instead of imitating others, focus on what best suits you and aligns with your capabilities and goals. In this essay, we will explore the importance of self-awareness, understanding limitations, and how embracing your uniqueness can lead to success and fulfillment.

The Temptation of Comparison

In today's hyper-connected society, we are constantly exposed to other people's successes through social media, news, and personal interactions. It's easy to feel pressure to emulate the achievements of others, especially when their accomplishments are widely celebrated.

For example, seeing a friend excel in a particular profession might prompt you to pursue the same career, even if it's not something you're passionate about. Similarly, watching influencers lead glamorous lives can lead to desires to follow in their footsteps, regardless of whether that lifestyle aligns with your values or abilities.

While comparing ourselves to others is a natural human tendency, it becomes problematic when it leads us to make decisions that do not align with who we truly are. Following the crowd or adopting someone else's path often ignores the uniqueness of our personal circumstances, values, and skills. What works for one person may not work for you because their success could be a result of specific talents, experiences, or resources that you do not possess.

The danger of comparison is that it can divert you from discovering and following your own path. Instead of focusing on what others are doing, it's crucial to focus on yourself and what you are capable of achieving. This requires a deep sense of self-awareness and the ability to recognize your own limitations and strengths.

Self-Awareness: The Key to Personal Success

Self-awareness is the foundation of personal growth and success. It is the ability to understand your own emotions, motivations, strengths, and weaknesses. Being self-aware means you have a realistic view of who you are and what you are capable of achieving. This knowledge enables you to make informed decisions that align with your goals, rather than chasing after someone else's definition of success.

When you lack self-awareness, you are more likely to be influenced by external factors, such as societal expectations or peer pressure. This can lead to poor decision-making, as you may end up pursuing goals that are not a good fit for your skills or interests. On the other hand, when you are self-aware, you can make decisions that are tailored to your unique circumstances and abilities.

1. Understanding Your Strengths and Weaknesses

One of the key components of self-awareness understands your strengths and weaknesses. Your strengths are the things you excel at—skills, talents, and abilities that come naturally to you or that you have developed over time. Your weaknesses, on the other hand, are areas where you may struggle or lack proficiency.

Knowing your strengths allows you to leverage them to your advantage. When you focus on what you do well, you are more likely to achieve success and feel fulfilled in your pursuits. Conversely, understanding your weaknesses helps you identify areas where you may need to improve or seek assistance. It also prevents you from overextending yourself by attempting tasks that are beyond your current abilities.

For example, imagine someone who admires a successful entrepreneur and decides to start their own business, even though they lack experience in management or finance. Without recognizing their limitations, they may encounter challenges that they are ill-equipped to handle, leading to failure. However, if that person were self-aware, they might recognize that while they are passionate about their business idea, they need to gain more experience or seek mentorship before launching their venture.

2. Recognizing Your Limits

Understanding your limitations is not about doubting your abilities or setting low expectations for yourself. Instead, it's about being realistic about what you can achieve given your current resources, skills, and circumstances. Recognizing your limits allows you to set achievable goals that are challenging yet within your reach.

Some people may have the capacity to achieve extraordinary things because they possess certain advantages—whether it's financial resources, innate talents, or access to networks and opportunities. However, trying to emulate their success without taking into account your own limitations can set you up for disappointment.

For instance, a person may be inspired by a marathon runner and decide to train for a race, even though they have no prior experience in long-distance running. If they push themselves too hard without considering their fitness level, they could risk injury or burnout. On the other hand, if they recognize their limitations and gradually build their stamina through consistent training, they will be more likely to reach their goal safely and successfully.

Recognizing your limits also allows you to focus on areas where you can grow. Rather than seeing limitations as barriers, view them as opportunities for improvement. By acknowledging your current limitations, you can develop a plan to overcome them through learning, practice, and perseverance.

3. Embracing Individuality and Uniqueness

Everyone is unique, with different experiences, perspectives, and abilities that shape their journey. One of the most liberating aspects of self-awareness is the realization that you don't have to follow someone else's path to be successful. Instead, you can embrace your individuality and pursue goals that align with your personal strengths, values, and passions.

Embracing your uniqueness means recognizing that there is no one-size-fits-all approach to success. What works for someone else may not work for you, and that's perfectly okay. By focusing on your own path, you can find fulfillment and satisfaction in achieving goals that are meaningful to you, rather than chasing after someone else's version of success.

This mindset also allows you to avoid the trap of envy or jealousy. When you appreciate your own strengths and limitations, you can celebrate the successes of others without feeling the need to compete or compare yourself to them. You understand that their achievements do not diminish your own potential, and you are free to pursue your goals at your own pace.

4. Setting Realistic and Meaningful Goals

Another benefit of self-awareness is the ability to set realistic and meaningful goals. When you have a clear understanding of your strengths, limitations, and values, you can set goals that are aligned with your true potential. These goals should be challenging enough to inspire growth, but not so unrealistic that they set you up for failure.

Setting meaningful goals requires introspection and reflection. Ask yourself: What do I truly want to achieve? What are my passions? What are my long-term aspirations? Once you have a clear sense of your goals, you can create a plan that is tailored to your abilities and resources.

For example, if your passion is writing, but you find that you struggle with time management, a realistic goal might be to write a certain number of pages each week, rather than trying to complete an entire novel in a short period. By setting achievable goals, you are more likely to maintain motivation and avoid the frustration that comes from setting unattainable expectations.

Avoiding the Pitfall of Imitation

One of the dangers of imitating others is that it can lead to a loss of authenticity. When you try to mimic someone else's actions or choices, you may end up abandoning your own values and desires. This can result in a sense of emptiness or dissatisfaction, even if you achieve some level of success.

Imitation can also lead to burnout. When you pursue goals that don't align with your true self, you may find it difficult to stay motivated or passionate about what you're doing. Over time, this can lead to frustration, stress, and a lack of fulfillment.

To avoid the pitfall of imitation, it's important to stay true to yourself. This means making decisions based on your own values, interests, and strengths, rather than following someone else's lead. It also means being patient with yourself and recognizing that your journey is unique. Success doesn't happen overnight, and it's important to stay focused on your own path, rather than constantly comparing yourself to others.

Practical Steps to Embrace Your Own Path

1. **Self-Reflection:** Take time to reflect on your strengths, weaknesses, and values. What are your passions? What are your long-term goals? Understanding these aspects of yourself will help you make informed decisions that are aligned with your true potential.

2. **Set Personal Goals:** Set realistic and meaningful goals based on your abilities and resources. Focus on incremental progress and celebrate small victories along the way.

3. **Avoid Comparison:** Resist the urge to compare yourself to others. Recognize that everyone's journey is different, and what works for one person may not work for you.

4. **Seek Support:** Surround yourself with people who understand and support your unique path. Mentors, friends, and family can provide valuable guidance and encouragement as you pursue your goals.

5. **Embrace Growth:** Recognize that limitations are not permanent. With effort and perseverance, you can overcome obstacles and grow into new areas of strength.

Conclusion

In a world where comparison and imitation are common, it's easy to lose sight of your own strengths, limitations, and uniqueness. However, success is not about following someone else's path—it's about understanding your own potential and making decisions that align with your capabilities and values. By cultivating self-awareness, recognizing your limits, and embracing your individuality, you can achieve success on your own terms. Instead of chasing after someone else's goals, focus on what best suits you, and you will find greater fulfillment and satisfaction in your journey.

XXXIII

Final Verdict: Becoming Your Best Version by Overcoming the Enemies Within

The journey to self-improvement is often seen as a battle—one where the most challenging and relentless enemies are not external forces but rather the ones residing within us. These inner foes include self-doubt, fear, ego, laziness, insecurity, and negative habits. They conspire against our progress, keeping us from reaching our full potential. However, the true victory comes not when we defeat others but when we conquer these internal obstacles and emerge as a better, more refined version of ourselves.

This essay delves into the concept of overcoming inner enemies, understanding the complexities of this battle, and finally, how this endeavor leads to self-mastery and personal transformation. The final verdict is that when you overcome these enemies within, you don't just win the battle—you become a stronger, wiser, and more capable individual, a better version of yourself.

The Enemies Within

Before we can talk about overcoming inner obstacles, it's essential to identify what these enemies within us look like. These are not tangible enemies but mental, emotional, and psychological barriers that prevent us from achieving growth. They take different forms for different people, but a few common internal enemies affect most of us:

1. Fear

Fear is one of the most powerful enemies within. It manifests as fear of failure, fear of judgment, or even fear of success. It paralyzes us, making us hesitant to take action or try new things. Fear often tricks us into staying in our comfort zones, which prevents us from growing and evolving.

2. Self-Doubt

Self-doubt is another formidable foe. It's the voice inside your head that tells you that you're not good enough, that you can't achieve what you've set out to do. Self-doubt diminishes confidence and robs us of the belief that we are capable of more.

3. Ego

While self-doubt drags us down, ego has the opposite effect—lifting us to heights of false self-importance. Ego can distort our sense of reality, making us believe we are better than we are, leading to complacency. It prevents us from learning from others or from our own mistakes.

4. Laziness and Procrastination

Laziness and procrastination are enemies that thrive on inertia. They keep us from taking action when we should. Procrastination allows important tasks to be delayed, often indefinitely, leading to missed opportunities and stagnation in our personal and professional lives.

5. Negative Habits and Addictions

Habits form the foundation of our daily lives. When we cultivate positive habits, we set ourselves on a path toward success. However, negative habits, such as poor time management, lack of discipline, or addictions to unhealthy behaviors, act as significant barriers to self-improvement.

6. Insecurity

Insecurity is rooted in a lack of self-worth. It causes us to constantly seek validation from others, making us vulnerable to external opinions and judgments. Insecurity breeds jealousy, competition, and an unhealthy need for approval, which can distract us from focusing on our personal growth.

7. The Inner Critic

The inner critic is the voice in your head that constantly judges, criticizes, and belittles you. It undermines your confidence and sows seeds of self-doubt. This inner voice is often harsher than any external critic and can be one of the toughest enemies to silence.

Acknowledging and Facing the Inner Enemies

The first step toward defeating these inner enemies is acknowledging their existence. Many people go through life unaware that their biggest obstacles are internal. They blame external circumstances, other people, or bad luck for their lack of progress. However, true growth begins when you turn inward and recognize that your greatest adversary is often yourself.

Facing these enemies requires self-awareness and brutal honesty. It involves looking in the mirror and admitting that fear, ego, laziness, or self-doubt are holding you back. This process can be uncomfortable, but it is necessary for personal transformation. Only by identifying these inner obstacles can you begin the work of overcoming them.

Strategies for Overcoming the Inner Enemies

Once you have identified the enemies within, the next step is to develop strategies for overcoming them. This process requires discipline, patience, and a commitment to personal growth. Here are some strategies that can help you defeat the inner adversaries and emerge as a better version of yourself:

1. Cultivate Self-Awareness

Self-awareness is the cornerstone of self-improvement. To overcome the enemies within, you must first understand how they operate in your life. Keep a journal to track your thoughts, emotions, and behaviors. Reflect on situations where fear, ego, or laziness took control, and analyze how you can respond differently in the future.

Meditation and mindfulness practices are also powerful tools for developing self-awareness. These practices help you become more attuned to your thoughts and emotions, allowing you to observe them without judgment. Over time, you'll become more adept at recognizing when your inner enemies are at play and taking steps to counter them.

2. Replace Fear with Courage

Fear will always be a part of life, but it doesn't have to control you. The key to overcoming fear is to act in spite of it. Courage is not the absence of fear but the decision to move forward despite being afraid. Start by taking small steps outside your comfort zone, gradually pushing the boundaries of what you're willing to do.

Visualization is another effective tool for overcoming fear. Imagine yourself successfully completing the task or goal that you're afraid of. This mental rehearsal can help reduce anxiety and build confidence in your ability to succeed.

3. Challenge Self-Doubt

To defeat self-doubt, you must learn to challenge and reframe the negative thoughts that fuel it. When self-doubt arises, ask yourself whether there is any evidence to support the belief that you're not capable. Often, you'll find that these doubts are based on irrational fears rather than facts.

Building self-confidence also involves taking action. Each time you accomplish something, no matter how small, you reinforce the belief that you are capable. Over time, these small wins accumulate, gradually eroding self-doubt and building a foundation of confidence.

4. Keep Ego in Check

Ego can be a destructive force if left unchecked. One of the best ways to keep your ego in balance is to practice humility. Recognize that there is always more to learn and that others may have valuable insights to offer, regardless of their status or position.

Receiving feedback is another way to combat ego. Be open to constructive criticism, and view it as an opportunity for growth rather than a personal attack. Surround yourself with people who are willing to challenge you and hold you accountable.

5. Build Discipline to Overcome Laziness

Discipline is the antidote to laziness and procrastination. It involves taking consistent action, even when you don't feel like it. One effective way to build discipline is by creating routines and sticking to them. Set specific goals, break them down into manageable tasks, and create a schedule to ensure that you stay on track.

Accountability can also help you overcome laziness. Share your goals with someone you trust, and ask them to hold you accountable for taking action. Regular check-ins can provide the motivation and support you need to stay disciplined.

6. Replace Negative Habits with Positive Ones

Breaking negative habits requires conscious effort and commitment. The first step is identifying the triggers that lead to the negative behavior. Once you understand these triggers, you can work on replacing the negative habit with a positive one.

For example, if you tend to procrastinate by scrolling through social media, you might replace this habit with a productive activity, such as reading or working on a personal project. Over time, the new habit will become ingrained, and the old one will lose its hold on you.

7. Practice Self-Compassion to Silence the Inner Critic

The inner critic thrives on negativity and harsh self-judgment. To silence this voice, you must practice self-compassion. Treat yourself with the same kindness and understanding that you would offer a friend. When you make a mistake, instead of berating yourself, acknowledge that it's part of the learning process and an opportunity for growth.

Mindfulness can also help you quiet the inner critic. By staying present and observing your thoughts without judgment, you can create distance between yourself and the critical voice in your head. This allows you to respond to challenges with greater clarity and calmness.

The Transformation: Becoming Your Best Version

When you commit to overcoming the enemies within, you set yourself on a path of continuous growth and self-mastery. Each victory over fear, ego, laziness, or self-doubt brings you closer to becoming your best version. Here's what that transformation looks like:

1. Increased Confidence

As you overcome self-doubt and fear, you will notice a growing sense of confidence in your abilities. This confidence is rooted not in arrogance but in the knowledge that you are capable of facing challenges and overcoming them.

2. Greater Resilience

Overcoming inner obstacles builds resilience. You become better equipped to handle setbacks and challenges because you've already conquered the toughest battles within yourself. This resilience allows you to bounce back from failures and keep moving forward.

3. Improved Focus and Productivity

When you defeat laziness and procrastination, you become more focused and productive. You are no longer held back by inertia, and you can accomplish more in less time. This increased efficiency allows you to make steady progress toward your goals.

4. Emotional Stability

Conquering the inner critic and practicing self-compassion lead to greater emotional stability. You are no longer at the mercy of negative self-talk or external validation. Instead, you have a strong sense of self-worth that remains constant, regardless of external circumstances.

5. Stronger Relationships

As you keep your ego in check and practice humility, you'll find that your relationships with others improve. You become more open to learning from others, more willing to listen, and more capable of forming meaningful connections.

6. Alignment with Your True Self

Ultimately, the greatest benefit of overcoming the enemies within is that you become more aligned with your true self. You shed the layers of fear, ego, and insecurity that once held you back, allowing your authentic self to emerge. This alignment leads to a sense of inner peace and fulfillment that can only come from living in harmony with your true nature.

The Final Verdict: Victory over the Self

The final verdict is clear: when you conquer the enemies within, you become the best version of yourself. This transformation is not easy—it requires discipline, self-awareness, and a commitment to personal growth. However, the rewards are immense. You gain confidence, resilience, emotional stability, and a deeper sense of purpose. Most importantly, you achieve mastery over the one person you have the most control over: yourself.

In the end, the battle against the inner enemies is the most important fight you will ever face. It is a battle that requires courage, patience, and perseverance. But when you emerge victorious, you will find that the greatest reward is not the absence of these enemies, but the strength, wisdom, and self-mastery you gain along the way. This is the true essence of becoming your best version—the final verdict of a life well-lived.